W9-BEZ-383

Artists' Gardens

17

Artists' Gardens

Bill Laws

Trafalgar Square Publishing

First published in the United States of America in 1999 by
Trafalgar Square Publishing, North Pomfret, Vermont 05053

Printed and bound in Hong Kong

Edited by Caroline Ball
Picture research by Poppy Owen at Image Select International

Library of Congress Catalog Card Number: 98-89408

ISBN 1-57076-147-7

Contents

Introduction

Artists respond to their local landscapes in different and quite individual ways. For Paul Cézanne and his contemporary, Gustave Caillebotte, the garden was both a workplace and a retreat; for Henry Moore and Barbara Hepworth it was a gallery. William Morris and John James Audubon used their gardens as a source of subject matter, while the Spanish Impressionist Joaquín Sorolla created for himself an evocative Moorish *patio*. Give an artist a plot of land and what Patrick Heron calls the 'painterly consciousness' comes into play, so that the artist cannot pass through a garden without instinctively framing, and often correcting, the view. If beauty is in the eye of the beholder, then composition lies in the eye of the artist.

Some artists paint what they see. Others paint what they feel. 'I know I can't paint nature, but I enjoy struggling with it,' Pierre-Auguste Renoir once confided to a friend. The Canadian painter Kim Ondaatje spoke of treating her garden 'like a blank canvas, deciding what to do with each part, but having a strong feeling about its ultimate outcome'; Gertrude Jekyll, once she had abandoned painting, devoted herself to creating gardens where 'every plant or group of plants shows a series of pictures'.

Good artists, however, do not necessarily become good gardeners. The American Impressionist Childe Hassam relied on the inspirational garden of a friend, the poet Celia Thaxter, for his vibrant paintings, while Claude Monet's neighbour Frederick Frieseke was as dependent on his wife's green-fingered skills as Renoir was on the *paysanne* qualities of his wife Aline. It begs the question: why celebrate the gardens of artists, rather than, say, those of the statesman or the station master, the former guaranteed to give a good civic show, the latter renowned for presenting passengers with a colourful border or two?

Apart from the historic links between art and gardening (in ancient China the two were almost inseparable, an Eastern link still clearly visible in the minimalist sculpture gardens of Isamu Noguchi), and the pervasive influence on garden design of artists such as William Kent, Humphry Repton, Morris and Jekyll, visual artists tend to compose imaginative and remarkable gardens. They are disinclined to suffer a foolish garden gladly – Monet, for example, could not abide the dull garden he first found at Giverny – and the artist gardener can be counted upon to spring a few surprises: witness the Swedish artist Carl Milles' capricious water sculptures, the innovative terraced town garden of Jennifer Bartlett and the cryptic layout of Emil Nölde's garden in Germany. And artists' gardens often have a tale to tell about the artists themselves: Rubens was revealed as an enthusiastic participant in the seventeenth-century mania for tulips; Heron uncovered the deep links between his windswept Cornish seascape and his bold, beautiful paintings; Ondaatje's organic husbandry and 'wild tame garden' paid homage to the teachings of a childhood Indian friend; and the native artefacts that surround the Mexican courtyard of Frida Kahlo's Casa Azul reflected her strong sense of national identity.

Within this book are painters and sculptors who soared to fame and others who slipped into obscurity. But almost all found themselves, at one time or another, at the cutting edge of artistic endeavour, striving against history, convention and fashion to express themselves in an original way. The shock of the new, whether it was the Impressionists of the nineteenth century or the Abstract Expressionists of the twentieth, sometimes confused the public and often enraged the critics who, in their time, have denounced them all.

Breaking boundaries is a lonely business and it was not surprising that so many artists should have chosen to retire from controversy and retreat into the private world of their gardens. Here, at least, there was no new thing under the sun, only fresh ways of seeing it. And ever since the Garden of Eden and its parallel Persian and Islamic paradise gardens, we have never grown tired of looking.

P i e r r e - A u g u s t e

R e n o i r

(1 8 4 1 – 1 9 1 9)

Pruned to provide a reachable harvest, the Mediterranean olive normally grows in neat, low rows. Left unchecked, the branches will soar skywards as the bole flares out and the roots writhe into strange shapes to consolidate their grip on the thin soil. The olive tree is a survivor.

'The olive tree, what a brute!' wrote the Impressionist painter Pierre-Auguste Renoir to a friend. 'If you realized how much trouble it has caused me. A tree full of colours. Not great at all. Its little leaves, how they have made me sweat! A gust of wind, and my trees' tonality changed. The colour is not on the leaves, but in the spaces between them.'

The source of so much artistic frustration was the gnarled, centuries-old olives which grew in Renoir's garden at Les Collettes in southern France. Planted in the days when local labour and long ladders were easy to find, these ancient trees had rarely been pollarded. About half of them survive to this day, their branches towering into a cool canopy, their exposed roots distorted into extravagant, sculptural forms. But for Renoir's intervention, all would have been put to the axe long ago.

Renoir spent the last eleven years of his life at Les Collettes, settled at last after a restless lifetime of moving from place to place. Looking increasingly gaunt and cadaverous, the result of an illness contracted during his spell of service in the French cavalry during the Franco-Prussian war, his health was deteriorating. The grey cold of the French winters exacerbated the rheumatism he suffered following a cycling accident ten years earlier. No amount of treatment at spas like St-Laurent-les-Bains and Bourbonne lessened the pain;

Dawn breaks over the garden at Les Collettes (left), the Provençal smallholding where the painter Pierre-Auguste Renoir lived for the last years of his life. Renoir rescued the garden, with its olive trees and yucca plants, from redevelopment, and painted it almost every day.

only painting seemed to bring relief. 'I just let my brain rest when I paint flowers,' he once told a friend.

In 1906, while he and his wife Aline wintered in a little house with a garden in the centre of Cagnes-sur-Mer, Renoir learned that the smallholding of Les Collettes was to be sold and its ancient olive grove felled to make way for a market garden. Curious, Renoir summoned his gardener-chauffeur, Baptistin, and together they drove out of town to the property. Cagnes-sur-Mer lies on the Riviera, the 40 mile (70 km) strip of coast that stretches from the one-time fishing village of Cannes to the Italian border. Carpeted in opulent villas, expensive hotels, hot tarmac and clipped, formal public gardens, the Riviera is a brash testament to the excesses of tourism. In Renoir's day it was still a busy place compared to the rough, beautiful Provençal countryside that lay just inland. The Provençal interior was a different world. Lines of vines simmered under their mulch of limestone shale. The low hills were clad in olives, the little fields, baking under the sun, were filled with a haze of scented plants grown for the perfumeries at Grasse.

Les Collettes and its 9 acre (3.5 ha) smallholding lay on a south-facing slope with a view across to

the Mediterranean sea. It was a conventional working farm with a terracotta-tiled gardener's cottage and traditional farmhouse, an olive, orange and citrus grove, a copse of oak and umbrella pines, productive vegetable plots and blushing bursts of oleander and pelargonium blooms. It was also bathed in the pellucid light which sparkled off the Mediterranean, a light whose quality captivated a host of artists including Pierre Bonnard, Paul Cézanne, Pablo Picasso, Henri Matisse, Raoul Dufy and Joan Miró, all of whom eventually settled on the Riviera. Like them, Renoir was drawn to the light like a moth to a candle flame.

Renoir was also drawn to Les Collettes during that first visit. The peace of the place settled on him like a comfortable old jacket, while the threat to the ancient

The olive tree is 'sad in grey weather, resonant in the sun and silvered in the wind,' wrote Renoir. He celebrated the ancient trees at Les Collettes (right) in many paintings, including 'Paysage Autour de Cagnes' (above).

olives touched a raw nerve. He had once bought a house at Essoyes, Aline's native village in the Aube region, but, for Renoir, the place was spoiled by the proximity of a fearsome saw-mill. The painter was a born conservationist – according to his son, the film maker Jean Renoir, his father used perform a curious little dance when he walked the fields to avoid crushing even the humble yellow *pissenlit*. The fate of the old olives lay in his hands: Renoir promptly bought Les Collettes.

Les Collettes remained an easy-going, relaxed farm garden, a refuge for agapanthus and lavender, for swathes of bearded iris and bamboo, for stands of cypresses, umbrella pines, palms and a magnificent strawberry tree (*Arbutus unedo*). Renoir knew all about the formal Italian garden styles from his painting trips. He was familiar, too, with Monet's exuberant creations at Giverny (see page 134), but he steadfastly resisted the temptation to domesticate or gentrify the garden at Les Collettes. Although he did once plan a formal garden centred around his sculpture, the Venus Victrix, it never came to fruition.

Aline, his former model and lover and later the mother of his three children, judged the farmhouse too unprepossessing for her dear, great Renoir, as she conventionally called him. There was a brief battle between husband and wife to have the old *mas* replaced with a more suitable, architect-designed residence. In the end, both had their way. The farmhouse was to stay – Renoir often included it in his pictures – and a new house was built close to the big linden or lime tree. But Renoir never painted it.

Aline, meanwhile, laboured to bring the garden to fruition, planting, pruning, manuring and harvesting according to the seasons. A resourceful vintner's daughter, she managed the goats, rabbits and hens, saw to it that the permanent artichoke beds were well hoed and that the annual harvest of orange blossom fetched a sensible price at the scent factory in Grasse.

She manured with grape skins the tumbling terraces of formal borders that fell away from the front door and she proudly bore the first pressing of their olives back to the house for a ceremonial tasting.

Renoir did create simple textural blocks of colour, underplanting with sprigs of santolina the white and pink oleander that lined the track to the house and planting thick drifts of irises that burst into mauve and blue bloom every spring. But for the most part he dictated the management of the wilderness garden, his master plan being simply to maintain the fruitful peace and tranquillity of a working farm and market garden. No gardener would mow the grass or weed a path without

*Renoir was going to create a formal garden around his 'Venus Victrix' (opposite), but his plans came to nothing. Instead he was content to keep a relaxed, informal garden where ivy-leafed pelargoniums and drooling datura (*Brugmansia*) flourished (above).*

seeking the master's permission and Renoir allowed the cycle of the seasons to revolve in the grassy tresses of the olive grove where the mustard and poppy, daisy and sorrel, lavender and marigold flowered and self-seeded themselves. This natural cycle – germination, flower, fruit and seed – sustained his work and accorded with his own view of life. The world, his garden and his work, as he saw it, was composed of interdependent parts and its equilibrium relied on its every part. 'When I paint flowers, I establish the tones, I study the values carefully, without worrying about losing the picture,' he once told a friend. For Renoir the painter, the managed disorder of a garden was a natural resource. 'If you paint the leaf on a tree without using a model you risk becoming stereotyped,' he was quoted as saying. 'Your imagination will only supply you with a few leaves whereas Nature offers you millions, all on the same tree. The artist who paints only what is in his mind must very soon repeat himself.' Given a free rein, Aline might have tried to tame and tidy Les Collettes. Instead she was content to compose her heavily scented, formal borders, nurture her roses and turn her green-fingered skills on the greenhouses and cold frames devoted to providing an all-year round supply of fruit and blooms for Renoir's still lifes.

He painted a small number of landscapes under the crystal clear Provençal light, although, since he loathed the cold, he rarely painted any in winter – 'Even if you can stand the cold, why paint snow? It is one of nature's illnesses,' he once remarked.

Renoir's excellence was as a portrait painter. Despite the critics (one described 'Torse de Femme au Soleil', a sensual, outdoor nude which sparkled with light, as a 'pile of decomposing flesh') the female form remained his favourite subject. 'Paint with the same joy you feel when making love to a woman,' he advised one young painter. Renoir would work in his garden studio painting Gabrielle, Aline's niece and maid, or some village woman who had been persuaded to pose for him, lying on the grass outside beneath the shade of the great, grey olive trees. And what inspired him, and gave him the light and tones he needed for the flesh colours of his nudes, was the rose.

From the age of thirteen Renoir had earned his first *sous* as an apprentice painting rose borders on saucers and plates in a porcelain factory and in his later

years he regularly used a rose from the garden for the daily vignette he would paint as a preliminary exercise to tackling a more arduous piece. In larger works such as 'Baigneuses' he might include a rose as a symbol of sensuality and to enhance the heavy beauty of a favourite model such as Gabrielle. 'Baigneuses' was an important work which Renoir himself described as a synthesis of all the experiments of his lifetime and the picture which laid the groundwork for his future work. Here in 'Baigneuses' are the elements of Les Collettes: the milky blue backcloth of the Provençal hills, the shading olive trees and, beside the creamy pink elbow of the foreground nude, a great, blowsy rose tucked into the band of a straw hat. No wonder the Provençal rose breeders, whose classic rose 'Peace' would mark the war's end in 1945, presented Pierre-Auguste with his own variety, 'Painter Renoir', in 1909.

By the time he and his family first arrived at Cagnes-sur-Mer, Renoir, once a poor Parisian factory worker, was a respected old man, doyen of the arts establishment and a bosom friend of Claude Monet. 'Without my dear Monet, who gave us all courage, we would have given up,' he once said. Artists such as Amedeo Modigliani, Chaïm Soutine and Henri Matisse beat a path to the painter's door to pay their respects to the man. For all his fame and fortune, Renoir continued to work like a man possessed.

Under the inspiring influence of Les Collettes, Renoir completed more than 500 pictures in this, his Iridescent period. This was the time that brought together his Impressionistic celebration of light and his classical sense of composition. He also embarked on sculpture for the first time in his life, producing pieces such as the voluptuously beautiful bronze 'Venus Victrix',

see page 13, a work which, in its turn, would inspire and influence Pablo Picasso.

In 1915, after their son Jean was severely wounded in the First World War, Aline died from the trauma. Without her *paysanne* qualities Les Collettes began to grow wild and unkempt. Renoir, his health deteriorating, knew he too was fast approaching death. Still he painted and painted. Arthritis crippled his hands and the loyal Gabrielle would bandage them with gauze,

It was Renoir's wife, Aline, who tended plantings such as the iris beds (above) and orange lantana and blue agapanthus (above right). The garden's swathes of pale blue 'Aline' irises, still there today, commemorate her skills.

Although Aline persuaded Renoir to build a new house at Les Collettes, he stubbornly refused to paint anything but the old mas *(opposite) that had been there when they arrived.*

slip a paintbrush between his fingers and, having prepared his palette, take him out into the garden to continue work. In November 1919, in his seventy-eighth year, Renoir caught a chill while painting in his garden. On Sunday 30 November, he began work on a still life of two apples. Early on the Wednesday morning he died, lying in Aline's bedroom on the first floor of the house at Les Collettes, two of his sons, Jean and Claude, at his side and his favourite dog Zaza at the foot of his bed. Through the open windows lay one of his favourite panoramas: the blue Mediterranean in the distance and, in the foreground, the umbrella pine grove, the citrus orchards and rose gardens of Les Collettes.

Now owned by the town of Cagnes and open to the public, Les Collettes not only has on display many of Renoir's paintings and sculptures, but still possesses the old olive trees that gave the painter so much trouble, and so much pleasure.

Henry

Moore

(1898–1986)

A wartime bomb landing on north London led Henry Moore, Britain's best-known twentieth-century sculptor, to rediscover the peace and tranquillity of the English country garden. In the First World War Moore had served as a teenage soldier and been gassed at the battle front in France. In the Second World War he was working as an official war artist for the government and in 1940, while he was sketching blitz victims sheltering in London's underground stations, his own home and studio in Hampstead were damaged during a German bombing raid. Henry Moore, then in his early forties, and his wife Irina were having a difficult war; materials were almost impossible to acquire and the art market was depressed. The bombing of the Moores' home was the final blow which drove the couple to seek sanctuary out of London.

Born in 1898, the seventh child of a Yorkshire coal miner, Henry Moore had excelled at art as a child, but, until he was sent to war in 1917, he had been persuaded to take a safe teaching job at his old school. When the war ended he used his army pension to pay his way through art school, first locally in Leeds and then in London at the Royal College of Art. By his mid twenties he was Professor of Sculpture at the Royal College. By his mid thirties he was ready to give up teaching altogether. He had met and married Irina Radetzky, a painting student at the College, studied ancient and classical art in France, Italy and Spain, held his first one-man show and made his first abstract piece of sculpture. The First World War had been a dangerous, but ultimately fruitful interruption in the life of the artist. The Second World War was proving to be simply dangerous.

A coal miner's son, sculptor Henry Moore challenged many of the artistic conventions of his day. The works in his garden (left) such as 'Goslar Warrior' and, in the distance, 'Three Piece Sculpture: Vertebrae', helped to make him the most widely exhibited sculptor in the world.

Henry and Irina moved to the countryside safely north of London and rented one of a pair of cottages at Perry Green, a hamlet near Much Hadham in east Hertfordshire. When Moore managed to sell a large elm wood sculpture of a reclining figure for £300, he raised just enough money for a deposit towards the purchase of both cottages, which were eventually joined together to make the home they called Hoglands. It was a sound investment: Henry and Irina would remain at Hoglands until Moore's death in 1986.

Hoglands in the 1940s, with its cottage garden, vegetable plot and surrounding grounds, stood on the edge of the hamlet. An old quarry bordered one meadow, ancient hedgerows filled with wild roses, blackthorn and hawthorn quartered the fields and native hornbeam, oak, ash and elm (until they were destroyed by Dutch elm disease in the 1970s) grew in quiet copses. The gardens and grazing land which had served generations of sheep farmers were in good heart and ready for change.

There are two opposing approaches to new garden design: that of the visionary and that of the

reformer. The visionary, armed with a personal plan and a sharp spade, will try to impose a design on the gardenscape; the reformer, having lived with the space for a season or two, will endeavour to tease out and highlight its natural features. Henry Moore had a foot in both camps. It was Moore the visionary who moved earth and rocks to create the small hill, often mistaken for a genuine Neolithic burial mound, which would serve as a viewing plinth for his large sculptures. But it was Moore the reformer who preserved the ancient hedgerows and trees and who created a natural network of grassy paths which meandered between his sculptures.

The sale of an elmwood carving allowed Henry Moore and his wife Irina to buy a pair of Hertfordshire cottages, Hoglands. As Moore's reputation grew, so did their estate, and every piece, such as the angular 'Knife Edge' (above) and 'Locking Piece' (opposite), could be given an appropriate setting and sufficient space.

Moore had had little time for gardening while he concentrated on his early career as a sculptor. However, he had always loved the outdoor life and freely admitted that his work was directly inspired by natural forms. 'Not to look at and use Nature in one's work is unnatural to me,' he said. 'It's been enough inspiration for two million years – how could it ever be exhausted?' One source of inspiration was the humble hedge. The Green of Perry Green referred to a Saxon clearing in the forests that once covered the area. The hedges that enclosed Hoglands were the last vestiges of these primeval woodlands and Moore regularly used to sketch the gnarled trunks of these hedgerow trees.

At Hoglands (the name referred to the swine that had once fed in the surrounding woods) Moore became one of the great exponents of the garden as a gallery, as he sited smaller pieces in the grounds and placed larger works in the informal setting of the surrounding fields. 'Some sculpture finds its best setting on a stretch of lawn or beside a pool. Others might be more effective, more poignant, set against the rhythm and raggedness of trees. Yet others need the secret glade, a patch of grass enclosed by high bushes to give a sense of privacy.'

Working in the grounds of Hoglands not only brought him closer to nature, but produced the challenge of working in ordinary daylight, especially the diffused, grey light of an overcast English day, the kind of light that, he thought, could inspire 'real sculptural power'. Acquiring Hoglands allowed him to work outdoors even in bad weather – he described working shut inside a studio as like being in a prison. While Irina cultivated the ever-expanding garden, managed the shrubs and flower beds and tended to the tree planting, Moore carried on creating pieces that excited and sometimes confused his public.

Placing these powerful forms in the grounds at Hoglands affected his relationship with his own, personal landscape. He professed to be hardly conscious of colour – 'I think it wouldn't hurt for a sculptor to be completely colour blind. In fact it would make him better, more able to concentrate on form and light without being intrigued or distracted by colour' – but he was acutely aware of the shape and lie of the land, of the light of the shifting seasons, even of the gradual growth

of the trees at Hoglands. Unlike the Japanese school of gardening which advocates the establishment of a finished garden and the process of snipping, clipping and pruning to maintain the garden's status quo, British gardeners relish the seasonal surge of growth. Moore was fascinated by the process. 'This asymmetrical response of trees and plants where there is insufficient space or sunlight has always interested me. If a tree needs more light, the branches will change direction; if a branch is cut off, it will be sealed and contained.'

In 1950, two years after winning the prestigious International Sculpture Prize at the Venice Biennale, the artist was still working from a single, small studio which had served as Perry Green's village shop. Thirty years later Moore had built nine different studios in what now extended to over 70 acres (30 ha) of ground. One, known as the Yellow Brick Studio, was where he did his woodcarving. Another, the only studio fitted with a carpet, stood beside the vegetable garden

'Mother and Child' (above) in a woodland setting and 'Family Group' (right) in a sea of blue flax: 'I am trying to add to people's understanding of life and nature, to help them to open their eyes and to be sensitive,' wrote Moore.

and served as his graphics studio. But perhaps the most significant of his workrooms was the maquette studio, which was filled with three decades of accumulated plasters, terracottas and found objects. Moore was an inveterate collector of *objets trouvés*, from flints and stones to fragments of bone. As a boy, he would return from a walk with his pockets stuffed with treasures – conkers, snail shells, strange leaves – which he would store and display in the family's garden shed. The maquette studio at Hoglands served the same purpose and became the place where Moore could transform his found objects into a hand-sized plaster maquette. In their turn these maquettes became the models for his powerful, full-sized sculptures.

As a young man walking in Adel Wood, a local beauty spot on the outskirts of Leeds, Moore made a special discovery when he chanced upon a great, bare boulder. 'For me it was the first big, bleak lump of stone set in the landscape and surrounded by marvellous gnarled, prehistoric trees. It had no feature of recognition, no element of copying of naturalism, just a bleak powerful form.' Before he and Irina arrived at Hoglands, Moore, still holding to that revelation, experimented with extremes of abstraction. By the beginning of the post-war period, however, he was retreating from the edge. Their daughter Mary, born in 1946, was still a toddler when the artist began work on his monumental 'Family Group', featuring an infant held in the entwining arms of a mother and a father figure. Completed in 1949,

The garden at Hoglands was used to site some of the smaller bronzes, such as 'Knife Edge Two Piece' (above) and 'King and Queen' (opposite). One critic described them as a menace from which the public should be protected.

'Family Group' was the first piece in which Moore depicted a male figure – until then he had concentrated on the figures of seated or reclining women – and, smoothed as weatherworn boulders, these great, calm figures were set on a simple bench in the grounds at Hoglands, their impassive gaze taking in the gentle agricultural landscape.

Larger sculptures were placed in the working landscape – 'Sheep Piece' (above) is particularly appropriately sited amid the grazing flock.

'There are a great many places that no sculptor has thought of – or has ever seen – that must be superb settings for sculpture,' suggested the artist.

For the visitor approaching Hoglands across the village green, however, there was not a sculpture in sight, only a glimpse of lawns and the high-gabled, seventeenth-century house itself. Behind the neat white fence, the willows and the shrubberies, Moore led a busy, but well-ordered life. It was Irina who created the garden areas where many of her husband's pieces were sited and it was Irina who, having tended the garden,

would prepare their one o'clock lunch. She expected punctuality. Meanwhile a growing staff, including sculpture assistants and gardeners, managed the insistent demands on England's busiest sculptor. Moore's work demanded lofty storehouses, storage areas, loading bays, lifts, cranes and lorries.

This hive of activity was built upon one pair of hands. These were the long fingers that moulded and measured (Moore always carried a tape measure in his pocket), that gripped the sculptor's tools or skilfully manipulated a penknife to draw the form from some hand-held plaster maquette. They were the hands that, in Moore's childhood, had massaged his mother's hip to relieve her sciatica pain and the hands which, for over forty years, speculatively framed the view and shaped the layout of Hoglands.

Despite the view of one critic who asserted that 'Mr Moore's work is a menace from which the public should be protected', Moore's works were more widely distributed across the globe than any other sculptor's. They could be seen at the Unesco headquarters in Paris, the Lincoln Centre in New York, the Gallery of Modern Art in New Delhi and the Henry Moore Sculpture Centre at the National Gallery of Ontario in Canada. Yet each piece owed something to the mood of the landscape and the feeling of freedom in the grounds at Hoglands. 'Sculpture gains by finding a setting that suits its mood, and when that happens, there is a gain for both sculpture and setting. My own garden is open, and almost merges with the Hertfordshire landscape, and I have noticed that even people who have no feeling for sculpture become aware of a kind of dislocation when a sculpture that they have been seeing pretty regularly in the garden goes away.'

Sometimes a sculpture was subtly changed by the way it was sited. His leviathan bronze 'Sheep Piece', for example, positioned on a grassy knoll in the field adjoining the garden at Perry Green, stood between a flock of sheep and their water trough. Moore was delighted rather than annoyed when the animals beat a track around the piece, their woolly backs burnishing a band of gold around the base of the sculpture as they rubbed against it.

Moore's sculptures added a futuristic dimension to the gardens of Hoglands, but in the 1950s and 1960s, as the ancient landscape of Hertfordshire gave way to gravel extraction, hedgerow destruction and urban development, Hoglands also became a rural sanctuary in the midst of change.

The Foundation that survived Henry Moore after his death now manages the estate and opens it to the public, giving visitors the chance to appreciate what Moore set out to do: 'I am trying to add to people's understanding of life and nature, to help them to open their eyes and to be sensitive. Nature', he added, 'is inexhaustible.'

Jennifer

Bartlett

(1941–)

Like anyone else, artists are often obliged to live in city surroundings, and those who regarded their gardens as essential to their lives usually managed to maintain some natural, green space close to their studio, Frida Kahlo, William Morris, Peter Paul Rubens and Joaquín Sorolla included. From the eighth-century Islamic paradise garden to the potted trees and false turf of the modern rooftop penthouse, the urban garden has always provided a retreat from the stresses of city life. But in the latter half of the twentieth century, when towns and cities dramatically expanded, garden designers sometimes trailed behind their architectural colleagues in devising innovative urban designs. The terraced gardens of the artist Jennifer Bartlett, however, opened a new chapter on the city garden. This exceptional garden, set on three levels of a converted railroad warehouse in Greenwich Village, New York, proved to be as radical as one of the artist's own paintings.

Designed to be as closely linked to the home's interior as they were to the complexities of their urban setting, the gardens, exposed to the harsh New York climate, were wedged between the surrounding buildings at the back of Bartlett's four-storey house. The conventional ground-level garden was laid down as a shaded, tree-filled area; a second garden, with its geometrically arranged flower beds and its water feature filled with fish, was built on the level above, beside the residential part of the home, and a third garden, with raised beds, heathers, grasses, shrubs and fruits, was constructed on the floor above.

Roof and terrace gardens have been slow to make their mark on the city scenery, despite research suggesting that the plants in these high oases significantly improve air quality. Bartlett's top garden, with its flower-rich plantings and sculptural plant forms, achieved a particularly intimate feel. A brick path led beneath a metal arch, framed with roses, ivy and wisteria, into a rose garden where the plants were separated by colour: yellow and cream, white 'Iceberg', and bright pink and scarlet. Close by stood a grapevine grown across a pergola and four raised beds filled with fruit trees and bedding plants such as stachys, geraniums, sedums and lady's mantle or alchemilla. Green, red and blue ornamental grasses were set in a long neighbouring planter box surrounded by small yews in square planters and scented honeysuckle, clematis and morning glory (*Ipomoea*) on iron climbers. The top garden was also home to the heather beds, which flowered in succession through the winter, and a shifting display of conifers, tulips, pansies, cosmos and dahlias, grown in pots and placed on the path intersections during their various flowering seasons. Finally a small, circular lawn was

The painter Jennifer Bartlett devised an extraordinary garden on several levels (left) which scaled the heights of her home in Greenwich Village, New York. The theme of the garden has risen repeatedly in her work.

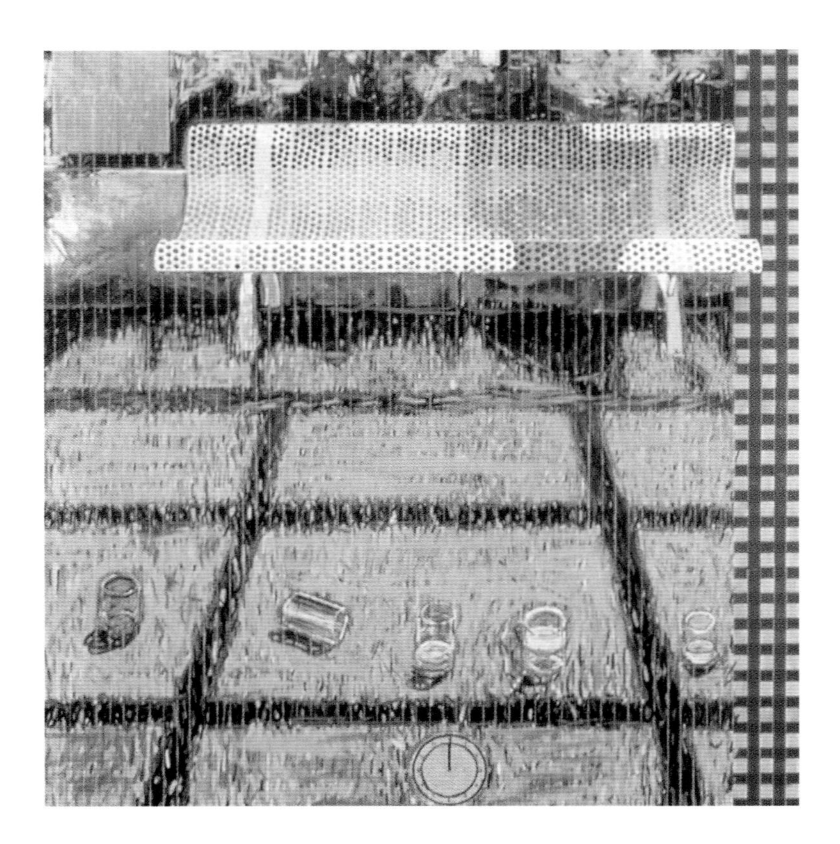

planted with a shrub garden that included camellias, blueberry, wisteria and espalier pears.

A spiral staircase connected the top garden to the second-floor garden below, where the sound of water trailing into a long water trough filled with aquatic plants and Japanese koi carp masked the sounds of the city. This garden was divided into eight beds by rectangular bars of clipped boxwood and sheltered by a tall screening wall climbed by wisteria and clematis. The flower beds, set out near seats flanked by Japanese white pines and low-growing evergreens, were planted with daffodils followed in summer by marigolds, impatiens, Japanese anemones and the daisy-like coreopsis.

Back in the ground-floor garden, meanwhile, a woodland glade of silver birch was left to soar skywards. Beneath the trees holly, astilbes, ferns, wild ginger and hostas shared the growing area with topiaried boxwood clipped into wave-like shapes. Every autumn

'Twelve Noon' (above) is one in Jennifer Bartlett's series of paintings entitled 'Air: 24 Hours', a personal tour of scenes in her New York home and city garden.

'Air: 24 Hours' took a year to complete, while the garden (right) was constructed within three weeks in 1991.

late-flowering cyclamen tubers produced a dash of colour in the shade garden.

Work on the construction of the gardens began in May 1991. Three weeks later the gardens, together with 40 tonnes of soil, their watering system and hundreds of trees, shrubs, annuals and perennials, were completed.

This Greenwich Village retreat was an extraordinary garden, constructed by an extraordinary artist. Jennifer Bartlett had decided on her career at an early age: when she was five she reportedly told her mother, a commercial artist and fashion illustrator, that she was going to be an artist and live in New York. She was right. Jennifer Bartlett was to become one of the most widely exhibited artists of her generation, renowned for the way she employed a large range of materials – pencil, ink, oils, pastels, collage, silk screens, even mirrors – to create elaborate representational works.

She was born in 1941, the oldest of the Losch family's four children, at Long Beach in California. She went to public school in Long Beach, quickly establishing herself as a non-conformist and an artist, although, while her art teachers praised her work, she was often at a loss to understand their reasons: 'I never understood why what I did was good.'

Her artistic direction took a more purposeful turn when she attended the Mills College in Oakland, the school in California which had strong associations with New York's Abstract Expressionists, particularly through artists such as Clyfford Still, Max Beckmann and Fernand Léger, who had all taught there. The Abstract Expressionist movement, which had developed in New York in the 1940s, saw artists covering their outsize canvases in expressive ways: they would use large brushes and even sprinkle or throw the paint at the canvas in the belief that the spontaneous approach could release an inner, unconscious creativity. Bartlett too began to experiment and in 1963, her senior year, she held her first one-woman show at the college.

She came under the influence of another group of experimental artists when her work at Mills secured her a place at the Graduate School of Art and Architecture at Yale. This school, under the direction of Joseph Albers, a former member of the influential German Bauhaus, had become a mecca for the more

adventurous students. A succession of guest artists – Willem De Kooning, Stuart Davis and Ad Reinhart among them – helped to orientate the school towards New York and its rapidly expanding art world, so much so that students like Jennifer Bartlett fully expected to be showing in New York before very long.

While Bartlett was studying at Yale and later teaching art at the University of Connecticut in Storrs, Connecticut, the social and political upheaval of the 1960s and 1970s was accompanied by a period of intense experimentation in the art world. Artists tried out new concepts, new styles and new ideas from minimalism and pop art to body art, conceptual art and earth art. As they searched out the new media, materials and images that would single them out from the crowd, Bartlett was seeking her own means of expression. She discovered the idea of substituting steel plates for conventional canvas. Like the signs in the New York subway, her plates, 1 ft (30 cm) square, were first coated with a layer of white baked enamel. She would then silk screen an image on to the plate and use enamel paints, sold in hobby stores for painting model aeroplanes and cars, limiting herself to four colours, red, yellow, blue and green as well as black and white. The paints were applied in the form of dots, placed in strict, mathematical combinations and progressions, and always following the same colour sequences.

In 1975, having laid in a supply of over a thousand steel plates, she began to plan a huge piece of work, a painting that would include both figurative and non-figurative images and which 'would have everything in it', as she put it. She adopted the geometry of the square, circle and triangle for the non-figurative images and, for the figurative images, a house, a tree, a mountain and the ocean. 'Rhapsody', as the work became known, was both an arduous and an experimental undertaking, but when it was exhibited at the Paula Cooper Gallery in New York it was not only well received by the critics, it was also promptly purchased by the art collector Sidney Singer. 'Rhapsody' gave Bartlett the confidence to continue and the following years saw her exhibiting in New York, teaching at the School of Visual Arts in downtown Manhattan and, travelling to Europe for the first time, exhibiting in London and Genoa. Bartlett, who was to become as well known in Tokyo and London as she was in New York, went on to a commission for Charles and Doris Saatchi in London, another for the Scientific Information in Philadelphia and a multi-part work, which included several large sculptures as well as paintings, for the Volvo Corporation's new headquarters. These were followed by two multimedia, multi-painting ensembles, 'Up the Creek' and 'To the Island', a pastels series, 'Sand Points', and set designs and costumes for the cinema and opera. In 1989 she completed 'The Fire' series and in the early 1990s, as she finished work on her New York garden, 'Air: 24 Hours'.

Over the years her body of work changed dramatically, becoming more powerful and resonant as time went by. Yet, as with Monet and Noguchi in their different ways, the theme of the garden repeatedly occurred in her work. During 1979 she traded living places with the writer Piers Paul Read and for a year settled in his villa at Nice in the south of France. She had planned to do no art work during her stay, instead travelling around Europe to study everything from Florentine Renaissance art to the

Although this clematis is healthy enough (opposite), the New York skyscape presents plants with a difficult and often harsh micro-climate.

'Two a.m.' (above), another in the 'Air: 24 Hours' series, features the ornamental grass garden and the artist's own hands.

Rosary Chapel at St-Paul-de-Vence in southern France, decorated by Henri Matisse. Although she had promised herself a rest, she could not resist taking a pencil and paper to the dining room table and beginning a series of drawings of the little garden outside. At the time it was a neglected area with a leaking swimming pool and five dying cypress trees, but Bartlett drew the garden repeatedly from every angle, producing nearly 200 drawings in different media and in styles which ranged from virtual abstraction to the meticulously realistic. In the bright light of morning and under the thin shadows of moonlight Bartlett drew the leaking pool, the unkempt perennials, the dark trees and even a kitsch statuette of a small boy urinating, so that when all the drawings, which became known as 'In the Garden', were exhibited together the work provided a narrative of her own curiosity and her voyage of discovery. Again in her commission for the London home of collectors Doris and Charles Saatchi, Bartlett, who had always had a consuming interest in interior design and furnishings, used the dining room walls of the Saatchis' home to picture the small, pooled garden outside in a variety of media.

A passing insect pauses to pollinate a rooftop cluster of heliopsis (above). City gardens like Jennifer Bartlett's (right), with its rose bowers and fragrant beds of catmint (Nepeta) help to clean the urban air and create a better environment for the city dweller.

She further explored the garden idea when she began the 'Luxembourg Garden' series. She and her husband Edward Bartlett had divorced in the 1970s and, by now married to the French film actor Mathieu Carrière, she was spending part of her year in a Paris apartment close to the seventeenth-century Luxembourg gardens. Working from snapshots of the gardens she built up two- and three-dimensional representations in materials ranging from pastel, brick and glass to wooden latticework and even Scots plaid.

One *New York Times* critic described her early 'Rhapsody' as enlarging 'our notions of time, and of memory and of change and of painting itself'. As her own work had risen from a ferment of styles and influences from Impressionism to Abstract Expressionism, so her garden rose from the sea of changing fashions which could be traced back even to the terraced gardens of Moghul India, where the lower level lay open to visitors, the second level was reserved for private and formal meetings and the top level served as a secluded refuge for the women of the court. Bartlett's New York garden showed what a resourceful artist could do to transform one small corner of the urban jungle.

Frida

Kahlo

(1907–1954)

Frida Kahlo painted herself again and again in a succession of self-portraits that detailed her development as an artist and as a woman. When she painted herself she invariably added some symbolic plant form or flower: the orchid as an emotional and sexual symbol; the wild acanthus to symbolize eternal life; and the thorned branches of a Mexican bush as an ancient reference to death and rebirth, in a self-portrait entitled 'Thinking About Death'.

In 1938, when she was commissioned by *Vanity Fair* publisher Clare Booth Luce to do a portrait of Dorothy Hale, a friend who had committed suicide, Kahlo executed a graphic painting of Dorothy Hale lying bleeding at the foot of the tower block from which she had thrown herself; pinned to her *femme fatale* black velvet dress was a dainty corsage of little yellow roses which had been given to her by a friend, and one of Kahlo's lovers, Isamu Noguchi. (Clare Booth Luce found the picture so upsetting she almost destroyed it.) When Kahlo executed a surreal portrait of horticulturist Luther Burbank, a man who had become famous for his fruit and vegetable hybrids, she pictured him as half man, half tree, his roots rising from the remains of a buried figure (see page 41) in one of her favourite themes of new life from death.

Yet another of Kahlo's plant motifs was the nopal, a cactus which features in the mythology of Mexico's beginnings and which flew on the Mexican flag. For Kahlo was a Mexican and an artist who identified herself so closely with the founding of the state of Mexico that she would give 1910, the year of the Mexican Revolution, as the year of her birth.

Frida Kahlo completed her 'Self Portrait with Monkey, 1938' (left) in a New York hotel, far away from Casa Azul, the Mexico home where she was born and where she would die. When photographed in 1939 (above), she was recently divorced from her husband, the painter and fervent nationalist Diego Rivera.

Magdalena Carmen Frieda Kahlo Calderón, the artist who signed herself Frida Kahlo, was actually born at her family home, Casa Azul, in Mexico City on 6 July 1907, three years before the Revolution. Surrounded by trees, the house still stands in a suburb of the city, Coyoacán, where it has served as the Museo Frida Kahlo since 1958, but the peace and tranquillity of the place belie the passionate life of the artist who lived and died here.

The cobalt blue walls that give Casa Azul its name surround an inner courtyard, a hothouse of trees, shrubs, succulents and potted plants intermingled with pre-Columbian sculptures and carvings stood on raised platforms and special shelves set into the walls. Overlooking this courtyard was Kahlo's studio, where her brushes, paints, portrait looking glass, her wheelchair and an easel holding an unfinished portrait of Stalin still stand. In one corner a glass case displays Kahlo's extravagant rings and necklaces; in another her embroidered blouse and the long, peasant skirt she often wore to conceal her leg, deformed by polio when she was six.

The rest of the house and a second garden area are filled with the ethnic pottery, masks, figures, toys and *retablos* – votive paintings of saints and martyrs – which Frida and her artist husband Diego Rivera collected. Kahlo never painted her Mexican garden or, if she did, her paintings have not survived.

Casa Azul had been built by her parents, Matilde and Guillermo Kahlo, in 1904. Matilde Calderón was of mixed Indian and Spanish descent. Her husband was a Hungarian Jew who had emigrated to Mexico from Germany in the 1890s and become a professional photographer. Under the Mexican dictator, General Diaz, Guillermo enjoyed a reasonable living, but when, in 1910, the Mexican Revolution upset the old order, times turned hard for the Kahlo family: Frida had to do shop-work after school to supplement the household income.

The Revolution lasted from 1910 to 1920 and Kahlo witnessed not only the street battles, but also the country's painful progress towards political stability. A committed socialist, she and Diego Rivera were active figures in its cultural revolution, which resurrected and celebrated Mexico's indigenous folk arts. While Rivera painted his murals and amassed the country's most

An inscription in the plant-filled inner courtyard of Casa Azul, the Blue House (above), records that Frida and Diego lived here: they were briefly divorced but remarried in 1940.

As a centrepiece to the garden Frida Kahlo and Diego Rivera built a scaled-down section of a pre-Columbian pyramid (right).

As in 'Two Nudes in the Forest' (above) Frida Kahlo often used exotic plant motifs in her richly coloured paintings. 'I have always painted with care, over and over, until the tones glow. The roots and vines of plants and flowers intertwine and find their way into the earth.'

important collection of pre-Columbian art, and Frida reclaimed Indian imagery for her paintings, the new *Mexicanos* explored every avenue of its arts and crafts – including gardens.

The conquering Spaniards had all but destroyed the royal gardens of Latin America in the sixteenth century, although surviving accounts spoke of exotic places where sophisticated canals and aqueducts were constructed to water the tree and fruit groves and, according to one historian, the 'gaudy family of flowers which belonged to the Mexican flora, scientifically arranged, and growing luxuriant in the equable temperature of the tableland'. In their place, the Spanish conquistadors introduced their own Moorish-influenced homes and gardens with their kitchen and fruit gardens and their private patios and shaded courtyards. When she was twenty-nine Frida Kahlo included her own Spanish-style garden as a background to 'My Parents, My Grandparents and I', depicting herself as a small child standing with her feet firmly planted in the

garden. In the picture an orange tree grows at her feet while her ancestral tree hovers above her head.

The cultural flowering of Mexico, and the work of Mexican artists such as Kahlo, captivated the art world in the early part of the twentieth century: Kahlo's first significant sale of work was to Hollywood star and art collector Edward G. Robinson. And when she was given a one-woman show in New York, her catalogue introduction was written by the revered French surrealist André Breton. She was to meet Pablo Picasso and Marcel Duchamp when thirty-two of her paintings featured in the Méxique exhibition in Paris; the Louvre purchased its first Mexican painting when it bought Kahlo's self-portrait, 'The Frame'. 'While I was swaggering through the streets [of Paris] the *imbecilio* French high fashion designers saw my long Tehuana skirts and petticoats, my ruffles, ribbons, and *rebozo*, and designed their own version: a dress named Robe Madame Rivera,' she wrote in her autobiography. 'The French people told me I was extravagantly beautiful. In Mexico, no one ever turned to look at me in the streets.'

When Casa Azul was extended, the new wing was built in grey volcanic stone (above). Diego Rivera set terracotta plant pots under the eaves and the garden was filled with pre-Columbian figures.

However, even at home, Frida Kahlo cut a controversial figure. 'To be like others is a bore. Even as a child I wanted to be distinct, to be different, to be adored.' For a time she cut her hair and dressed as a man, posing in a family photograph with her sisters in a dapper suit and carrying a cane. Later, like many educated Mexican women, she adopted the flamboyant dress of the Tehuantepec region of south-west Mexico, where a strong matriarchal tradition survived.

In 1925, the eighteen-year-old Kahlo was travelling home on the school bus when it struck a tram. Several people were killed and Kahlo, speared by a hand rail, was badly injured. She was not expected to live as she lay covered in blood and gold dust – another passenger's package of gold had broken open and its contents spilt across the injured. The accident shattered her pelvis, back and right foot and she was confined to her bed for months. Her father loaned her his paints, a carpenter constructed a special easel and the canopy of her bed was fitted with a full-length mirror. Kahlo began to paint. 'Painting was my only true medicine. It completed my life.'

Over the next twenty-eight years she would endure more than thirty-two operations. As she put it: 'I always knew there was more death than life in my body.' Despite the pain, the surgery, the steel casts and surgical corsets, Frida Kahlo lived a full and a passionate life. She met and married Diego Rivera, at that time the best known of the Latin American artists and twenty-one years her senior. Ten years later she divorced him for his womanizing – one of his affairs was with Kahlo's own sister – but in 1940 remarried him on the condition that they shared everything but money and a marriage bed. In a reaction to Rivera's philandering ways, Kahlo had affairs with others, including Leon Trotsky and the photographer Nickolas Muray. Throughout this turbulent career she painted herself with clinical, absorbed detail – her arched eyebrows, the pronounced down on her upper lip, her operations, even her miscarriages. 'The Frida that I have inside is only known to me. Only I can tolerate her,' she once wrote. For Kahlo there were two fixed points in this brief whirlwind of a life: her husband, transient and distinctly unreliable, and the solid familiarity of the Casa Azul and its garden. Although she lived briefly in San Francisco, Detroit and New York, she inevitably returned to her house and garden in Coyoacán.

Frida Kahlo taught herself to paint in her teens, following a crippling road accident. Her wheelchair (above) stands before her easel and an unfinished portrait of Josef Stalin.

Frida Kahlo's affectionate portrait of the horticulturist, Luther Burbank (right), shows him 'growing' out of a cadaver, symbolizing nature's powers of regeneration.

Before the Spanish conquest, Coyoacán, literally the Place of the Coyotes, had been a town on the shores of Lake Texcoco. Until Kahlo married Rivera in 1929, Casa Azul and its garden remained little changed as Coyoacán was gradually absorbed into the urban sprawl of Mexico City. While he maintained his own home nearby, Rivera had built a stepped pyramid in the centre of the *patio*, its steps lined with pre-Columbian sculptures. He then oversaw the addition of a new wing to accommodate extra studios and bedrooms. In contrast to the traditional blue stucco of the old house, the new wing was built in dark, pitted blocks of volcanic stone. As an afterthought he added a row of large terracotta pots, soon colonized by plants and pigeons, under the eaves of the roof.

A photograph taken in 1933 by Kahlo's father Guillermo shows the courtyard with its orange tree in the centre surrounded by waist-high borders set against the walls of the house and lined with pots of flowers. The traditional, sun-filled terrace with its truncated pyramid was retained, but a new garden was built to serve the extension of the house. Steps from the new wing led down to an open balcony built, not in some slender

Luther Burbank

Hispanic style, but with stout squared sections of stone. A flight of steps led from the balcony to a shaded recess beneath and a high-spouting fountain with a little Moorish-style pool before it. The temple-like niche under the balcony was filled with more ancient pre-Columbian sculptures. A garden, according to the Mexican designer Luis Barragán, should serve as the soul of the house and be a magic place for the enjoyment of meditation and companionship; if Casa Azul's traditional terrace harked back to Mexico's Spanish colonial days, this new 'soul of the house' was modernistic and sculptural. In 1952 Frida was photographed here, her Tehuana skirt spread out across the lower step, the impassive faces and stone figures of the pre-Hispanic figures surrounding her.

These were Frida Kahlo's final years – she died in 1954 – when she would paint in the garden or the studio, often in great pain and under heavy sedation from painkillers. In contrast to her intensely detailed and technically precise early works, her brushstrokes grew loose and inexact as she painted still lifes of fruits from the garden or the local market, inevitably adding symbolic touches such as a red, white and green Mexican flag plunged into an orange, or a dove of peace nestling among a collection of fruits and vegetables. 'The roots and vines of plants and flowers intertwine and find their way into the earth,' she wrote. 'Fruits become very tempting and lush.'

Sensing her imminent death, a friend organized Mexico's first one-woman exhibition of her work in 1953. Doctors forbade her to attend, but Frida, dosed up with painkillers and alcohol, had herself brought to the gallery in an ambulance. She attended the opening of the exhibition lying on a stretcher.

Kahlo died the following year, at only forty-seven, amid rumours that, suffering from so much pain, she had hastened her own death. After her cremation, Frida Kahlo's ashes were placed in a pre-Columbian urn and brought back to the place she was born, her faithful Casa Azul.

A cat slumbers above a bed of cannas in the garden where Frida Kahlo sought and found sanctuary from the pains and passions of her life. The last entry in her diary read: 'I hope the exit is joyful . . . and I hope never to come back.'

Gustave Caillebotte

(1848–1894)

'Is it known that the painter Caillebotte, who was a passionate gardener and boatsman, was also one of our most devoted collectors of postage stamps?' enquired one of Gustave Caillebotte's obituary writers at the artist's death in 1894. The writer failed to mention that the artist was also a collector, a generous patron of his fellow French Impressionists, a modest impresario, an investor in real estate and, in his later years, even the designer and builder of racing yachts.

His output as a painter encompassed a range of subject matter that mirrored the breadth of his obsessions and perfectly pictured the life and times of France in the late nineteenth century: he painted figures of workers and bourgeois city dwellers, townscapes, country views, bathing and boating scenes, landscapes, interiors, portraits, still lifes and decorative flower pieces. His works went on show at five of the Impressionist exhibitions. He supported his fellow painters, buying their works and championing the movement in the face of ridicule and disapproval. He was also a discerning collector who, in the course of an eighteen-year period, built up a remarkable and now priceless collection of paintings and pastels that contained some of the most resonant and outstanding images of the time. When he died Caillebotte left to the French nation sixty-five major works by Degas, Monet, Pissarro, Renoir, Cézanne, Sisley and Manet. (Extraordinarily enough, the state refused twenty-seven of the paintings.)

Caillebotte's enthusiasm for gardening, however, was equal to that of Monet and, in the last twelve years of his life, the artist devoted himself more and more to his garden. He was born into a wealthy family in Paris in 1848. His father, Martial, was involved in

A woman tends a voluptuous border of old-fashioned standard roses in full bloom in Gustave Caillebotte's 'Les Roses, Jardin du Petit Gennevilliers' (left). The artist purchased the house and garden at Petit Gennevilliers around the time he painted his self-portrait (above).

property development and managed lucrative contracts for the army. As a result, Martial Caillebotte could afford to run a substantial town house in Paris and a large country estate with parkland bordered by the river Yerres in what is now the Essonne region to the south-east of Paris. Caillebotte spent much of his youth in this eighteen-bedroom house with its luxurious garden, its greenhouses and pavilions and it was here that the young Gustave first developed his parallel interests in gardening and landscape painting.

Initially, Caillebotte trained as a lawyer and, after serving his apprenticeship, practised in Paris until, in 1870, he was drafted into the army to fight in the Franco-Prussian war. When the war came to an end Caillebotte abandoned his legal career and instead became a habitué at the studio of the establishment Salon painter Léon Bonnat. Bonnat took a liking to the young man and sponsored him for entry to the prestigious Ecole des Beaux-Arts. In 1873, Caillebotte passed the entry examination and a year later met Edgar Degas, Claude Monet and Pierre-Auguste Renoir. Although not a single one of his own paintings was shown, he helped them to organize the First Impressionist Group exhibition

in Paris. As time went by, Caillebotte played the role of benefactor and impresario for the group, locating and borrowing works, framing, hanging, organizing invitations and publicity. He was also generous with his money and gave financial assistance to both Pissarro and Monet in particular, paying their rent, settling their debts and helping them out with loans and advances.

When in April 1876 the Second Impressionist Exhibition took place, Caillebotte showed eight of his own paintings, four of which were inspired by the garden and domestic scenes from his town house and the family's country estate at Yerres. Stimulated by the contemporary passion for Japanese prints and the emerging art of photography, Caillebotte brought to these works the new Impressionist ways of thinking about composition and, at first, seen as a more traditional painter in the group, he met with critical approval. But by 1878, as he began to play with distorted perspectives and saturate his pictures with blue pigment, he became the recipient of the kind of public ridicule that had once been reserved for Renoir and Monet. Caillebotte began to fall from fashion.

From 1880 onwards Caillebotte fell victim to the shifting political and social change of the period. The communal spirit, which had once welded the Impressionist artists together, evaporated and as they each began to become successful in their own right, Caillebotte's role as their patron came to an end. The

Caillebotte came from a wealthy background, and it was on the family's large country estate at Yerres (above and right) where he developed a life-long passion for painting and horticulture. The artist's paintings were used as a reference when part of the estate, now a public park on the outskirts of Paris, was renovated.

artist grew weary and discouraged. He reined in his artistic ambitions, produced fewer paintings and instead devoted himself to horticulture. His passion for gardening, for growth and nurture, would sustain him until his death – finally it was his garden and not his art that preoccupied this resilient and energetic man.

After the death of Caillebotte's mother in 1879, the family estate at Yerres was sold. Two years later the artist acquired a house at Petit Gennevilliers on the banks of the Seine, north-west of Paris and across the river from Argenteuil. This had proved to be an inspiring landscape for Monet and Manet, who frequently set up their canvases to paint here, but for Caillebotte it was the river and the lure of boating that attracted him to the site.

A notary's document described Petit Gennevilliers as 'enclosed by grilles, trellises and earth embankments, and with a surface area of roughly 10,000 square metres and fronting on to the towing path from the Seine, and abutting at the back an earth embankment'. Like the houses of Renoir and Monet, the house and garden at Petit Gennevilliers was intended to reflect the artist's status. (While some critics still condemned Impressionism – one academic painter referring to it as 'filth' – artists from across the world were converging on France to pay homage to the new artists and to catch a glimpse of Caillebotte's growing collection.)

The new house was a typical, fashionable, contemporary residence, built of roughly textured stone and roofed with the latest industrially manufactured red tiles, but when it came to the gardens and studio Caillebotte shaped them to suit his own specialist needs. Apart from a large studio space, he planned a sizeable greenhouse, separate pavilion quarters for two gardeners, numerous outbuildings and specific planting plans. He even specified the design of his own garden

entrance gates, simple x-shaped, criss-crossed structures painted brilliant white.

The painter was already familiar with the principles of garden design. The family estate at Yerres had been laid out along the lines of an eighteenth-century landscaped English garden and, until it was sold, he had repeatedly studied it as he produced over sixty oil paintings and pastels. (Now a municipal park, part of the old family estate at Yerres is still under cultivation. Based on Caillebotte's paintings of 1877, a section of the walled kitchen garden has been planted out with vegetables, with neat rows of beans, lettuce, tomatoes and other crops. His house and garden at Petit Gennevilliers, however, were destroyed.)

The period when Caillebotte conceived his garden at Petit Gennevilliers coincided with radical developments in garden design. There was a growing reaction against the rigid geometric designs of the old order, a burgeoning interest in flower gardens and a technological revolution in gardening equipment and architecture. Gardeners and painters were experimenting with the ideas of Michel-Eugène Chevreul, his critical analysis of colour theory and his notions about complementary colours, ideas which Gertrude Jekyll was to find so profitable in her own work (see page 170). Caillebotte, too, was aware of Chevreul's ideas and how they could be used to dictate the choice of plant colours and the way in which flowers were arranged in their borders.

The garden at Petit Gennevilliers was arranged along traditional lines with rectangular flower beds, but organized so that each individual plant was allocated a specific place. Using the garden almost as an experimental laboratory, Caillebotte chose and propagated plants specifically for their colour and their flowering season. He kept up to date with new developments through his subscription to the *Revue horticole, journal d'horticulture pratique,* a publication that communicated the latest information about horticultural innovations and the discovery of new species. He even achieved some modest successes: at a meeting of the Société Nationale d'Horticulture in 1891 Paul Hariot reported having 'had occasion to admire at the home of M. Caillebotte, in Petit Gennevilliers, a very complete series of perennial poppies resulting from the cross-fertilization of *Papaver orientale* and *P. bracteatum*'.

The artist delighted in his collections of dahlias and roses, and nurtured new and rare orchid species in his special hothouse. He built the formidable greenhouse in 1888 and equipped it with a special hot-air stove to enable him to raise his orchids and other exotic plants. The greenhouse can be seen in two of

In contrast to the conventional French formality of the Caillebotte family garden at Yerres (above), the artist organized his new garden at Petit Gennevilliers as a trial growing ground for his roses, dahlias and orchids.

Caillebotte kept up to date with the latest developments in gardening, sharing his ideas on flower and vegetable growing (above and right) with Claude Monet. Sadly, Caillebotte's garden at Petit Gennevilliers does not survive.

Caillebotte's canvases as a brightly illuminated building viewed in full sunlight from a dark foreground of yellow dahlias and foliage.

Impressionist gardens often made the most of the dramatic effects produced by strong contrasts of light and shade and this fusion of nature and art was also evident in an island bed at Petit Gennevilliers where Caillebotte planted maroon and black pansies together with white and cream ones.

Along with Monet and other painters, Caillebotte shared a passion for the vogue for japonisme which swept through France in the late nineteenth century. One consequence of the cultural influence of the East was the popularization of the chrysanthemum, a favourite plant of many Impressionist painters and one that they frequently included in their still life arrangements. In the garden at Petit Gennevilliers Caillebotte cultivated a large number of these autumn-flowering Japanese perennials, in particular the variety commonly known as 'football' chrysanthemums with their heavy, rounded, crumpled heads. His canvas 'White and Yellow Chrysanthemums', which he presented to Monet, was painted in 1893, at a time when the two artists were engaged in lively exchanges of information about horticultural developments. The two men were also deeply interested in '*la décoration florale*', where the decorative qualities of the garden scene could be brought into the house to provide inspiring schemes for interior design. 'White and Yellow Chrysanthemums' was an example of Caillebotte's increasing enthusiasm for colour and coincided with his project to paint the door panels of his dining room with pale orchids and silver begonias set against the dark green foliage of his greenhouse.

There were yet more links between his art and his garden. For example, Caillebotte favoured strongly accentuated perspectives with sharp diagonals in his paintings. When he came to plant out his fruit trees, he combined aesthetics with economy and trained them to grow in similar formal, geometric patterns. Using fan, cordon and espalier methods and with skilful pruning, he trained the trees to grow along vertical poles, horizontal wires or low wooden supports. Since these structures saved space, many more trees could be planted and the fruit could be harvested more easily.

Caillebotte had much to do in his garden, but little time to do it. Although his father had lived to the age of seventy-seven, his younger brother, René, was only twenty-six when he died. Caillebotte, who drafted his first will when he was only twenty-eight, nominating money to provide for the next Impressionist exhibition and bequeathing his art collection to the French nation,

feared his family was fated to die young. In fact the artist, probably having suffered a stroke, died at his home in February 1894 at the age of forty-five. He had reportedly fallen ill while working in his garden.

Soon after his death Pissarro wrote: 'We have just lost another sincere and devoted friend . . . And he is one we can really mourn. He was good and generous and what makes things even worse, a painter of considerable talent as well.' France had lost a good painter: it had also lost a good gardener. In the spring of 1894, some days after the artist's death, the critic Gustave Geffroy arrived at Petit Gennevilliers to view Caillebotte's collection of Impressionist works. He was, however, equally intrigued by the organization and the complexity of the artist's garden, 'this little vegetal world that was labelled, pampered, adored by Caillebotte'.

Chrysanthemums (above) were a favourite flower in the Impressionist garden. Caillebotte's 'White and Yellow Chrysanthemums' (opposite) was painted at Petit Gennevilliers the year before he died.

William

Morris

(1834–1896)

Many artists only discover a garden 'where the soul's at ease', as the Irish romantic poet W. B. Yeats put it, in middle or late life. William Morris, an acquaintance of Yeats and one of the greatest English designers of all time, established his most inspirational garden at the age of twenty-six and enjoyed it for a mere six years. Nevertheless it was a garden that would shape all his future work.

William Morris was born on 24 March 1834 in what was then the country village of Walthamstow, on the outskirts of north-east London. His parents were wealthy, especially after his father (also called William), a successful stockbroker in the city of London, made a spectacular killing in some copper mine shares. The family moved to Woodford Hall, not far away, where William, their third surviving child, not only had the free run of a large estate, but also was given his own garden plot to cultivate.

William Morris senior was an enthusiastic medievalist who regularly took his son on trips to English churches and cathedrals, places where the boy learned to admire the architecture and classic craftsmanship, the fine stained glass, etched memorial brasses, woodcarvings and stonework. Long before he reached the dreamy spires of Oxford University, Morris had gained a thorough understanding of nature and a deep love of history.

Morris went to Oxford in 1852, a year after visiting the Great Exhibition in London's Hyde Park. The seventeen-year-old was not impressed. He was convinced that the Exhibition had been hijacked by the nation's industrialists and used as a vehicle to promote the outpourings of mass production. One story suggests he refused even to enter the Crystal Palace because he considered the works inside 'ugly'. For Morris, the mellow limestone of Oxford, the rushy banks of its boating rivers and the stimulating company of his tutors and students were far more alluring.

When William Morris was photographed at fifty (above), his garden at the Red House in Kent was no more than a sometimes sad memory. However, places like the bluebell-filled Rose Walk (left) had a deep influence on the artist who founded the English Arts and Crafts movement.

Morris proved to be a gifted, if not such a diligent, student and he devoured the contemporary writings of the day, especially those of Thomas Carlyle ('Man is a tool-using animal. Without tools he is nothing, with tools he is all') and John Ruskin ('The first duty of a State is to see that every child born therein shall be well housed, clothed, fed and educated . . .') Despite, or perhaps because of, his own inherited affluence, Morris found himself in complete accord with those who were critical of the machine-driven, materialist society. He met the painter Edward Burne-Jones, a man who was to become his closest friend and most inspirational collaborator. Soon the two men had joined a group of students who looked back on the pre-industrial past with nostalgia and who foresaw a time when the inspiration of the

artist would meld with the honest labours of the craftsperson. The concept of an arts and crafts movement was about to be born.

Morris travelled to Europe to inspect the medieval tapestries and Gothic cathedrals of northern France and Belgium, and returned to Oxford determined to abandon his original choice of a profession – the priesthood – for a second career in architecture. He joined a firm of Oxford architects, but lasted in their service only long enough to become firm friends with a fellow articled clerk, Philip Webb, and to affirm his instinctive enthusiasm for traditional crafts – ironwork, stained glass, stone and woodcarving and hand-printed fabrics and furnishings. 'Everything made by man's hand has a form, which must be either beautiful or ugly; beautiful if it accords with Nature, and helps her; ugly if it is discordant with Nature, and thwarts her,' he once said in a lecture.

Still the impetuous youth, Morris left the architectural practice to join his Bohemian friends in London, sharing rooms with his Oxford companion, Burne-Jones. The two men were to become part of the most influential team of artists and designers of the nineteenth century, but not before meeting Dante Gabriel Rossetti, the poet and painter who was to be the third, and most notorious, member of the group. Rossetti, like John Everett Millais and William Holman Hunt, was part of the secret Pre-Raphaelite Brotherhood of artists, whose methods and symbolic subject matter earned them censure – blasphemers, cried one critic – and praise: Ruskin described their work as 'noble'. The Pre-Raphaelites despised the pervasive influence of the old Italian masters who used bitumen, which blackens with age, to darken their tones. Instead they built up their bright colours and sharp detail on a wet white ground laid over their preliminary sketches. Morris was as captivated by their style as he was by Rossetti's young model, Jane Burden, the tall, aloof and strangely beautiful daughter of an Oxford stablehand. In 1859 Morris persuaded Janey to marry him. Only years later would she admit that she had never loved him.

Morris, meanwhile, experimented in almost every field of the arts and crafts, from poetry, prose, painting and publishing to furniture design, frescos, book illustration and binding and even the translation of Icelandic sagas. When he established a company of makers and designers, Morris, Marshall, Faulkner and Co., later to become simply Morris & Co. and dedicated to countering mass production with individually designed and hand crafted articles, Morris brought his naturalistic designs to each of the different crafts.

In the 1870s, Morris was producing wallpaper designs based on willow, larkspur and jasmine. In the 1880s he was experimenting with dyed and printed

William Morris filled many sketchbooks while at the Red House, detailing the climbing plants such as the clematis and honeysuckle (left) that covered the garden's trelliswork. One day these sketches would form the basis for designs such as his 'Trellis' wallpaper (above).

textiles, designing such popular lines as 'The Strawberry Thief'. Although new aniline dyes, cheaper and quicker drying than the old dyes, had come on to the market, he researched his earthy reds, yellows and shades of salmon and flesh colours from natural, vegetable dyes – 'very pretty it was to see silk coming green out of the vat and gradually turning blue.' When Morris and Co. came to design hand-blocked, printed fabrics, it was William Morris who drew the tracings of stylized tulips, honeysuckle, acanthus and African marigolds and supervised them being cut into the pear wood printing blocks. Occasionally the company produced embroidery designs which their wealthy patrons worked themselves; invariably Burne-Jones drew the figures while Morris added the decorative, plant-based backgrounds. Morris also used plant images in his weavings, carpets and tapestries. In 1897 he set up a loom in his bedroom and spent 500 hours making 'Vine and Acanthus', or 'Cabbage and Vine' as it became known, a rich embroidery of trailing vines and convoluted cabbage-like leaves which demonstrated not only a mastery of the medium, but the artist's eye of the plant world.

With his shock of hair and his wild beard, Morris was also a firebrand. He shocked Victorian society by becoming a revolutionary socialist, by turning down the position of Poet Laureate and, when founding the Society for the Protection of Ancient Buildings, by roundly condemning 'the spreading sore of London swallowing up with its loathsomeness field and wood and heath without mercy'. Morris, the middle-class rebel, adopted the working clothes and the life of the artisan and was often rude to his wealthy customers. Yet the prestigious *Titanic* set sail on its fateful maiden voyage equipped with luxury cabins decorated by Morris & Co. and, a century after his death, his craftsmanship could still send ripples through the world of contemporary design.

At his funeral in 1896, when a painted farm wagon wreathed with bulrushes and willow wands bore

A flower border at the Red House in early spring (right) demonstrates the influential Arts and Crafts character – Morris's reaction against the high Victorian style extended to a garden that celebrated crafts and old-fashioned plants.

his plain oak coffin into a Cotswold graveyard, the obituarists remembered Morris as a designer, poet, craftsman, writer and social reformer. (One of his physicians reportedly offered the cause of death as 'simply being William Morris and having done more work than most ten men'.) However, although his biographer J. W. Mackail noted that 'of flowers and vegetables and fruit trees he knew all the ways and capabilities', little credit was given to Morris the gardener, nor to the inspiration he drew from his Arts and Crafts gardens.

Morris kept a garden wherever he could. Kelmscott House, his London home by the Thames at Hammersmith, was named in honour of his Cotswold retreat, Kelmscott Manor, and its garden – Janey referred to its 'many paintable bits' – was laid out with gravel paths winding around a walnut and a tulip tree (*Liriodendron tulipifera*), horse chestnuts and a small orchard. He had little opportunity to advance the gardens at Kelmscott Manor, not least because, for a time, Jane Morris lived there with her lover, Rossetti. In fact Morris spent most of his life living in or close to London, and yet much of his work revolved around plant and flower forms.

Although he drew on his boyhood days in Epping Forest, his most intense period of study and observation came during the brief time he and Janey lived at the Red House. The Red House was designed by Morris's friend from Oxford, the quiet and introspective Philip Webb, who, when he received a commission, was in the habit of touring the district and interviewing local craftspeople on their vernacular techniques and materials. Built for Morris and his new wife, the Red House and its garden was his first solo commission and, like the Morris family and their friends Burne-Jones and Rossetti, Webb was eager to give it the full Arts and Crafts treatment.

Morris had found the site, a Kent orchard filled with apple and cherry trees near Bexley Heath, just beyond reach of the 'spreading sore' of London, and instructed Webb to design it so that scarcely a single tree would be felled. When the house was finished some fruit trees stood so close that windfall fruit regularly rolled in through its open windows. The L-shaped house was to be locked into the local landscape, the hand-made red bricks used for the walls repeated in the paths that led out into the garden and on a tall well-tower which was set as a centrepiece in the courtyard. Conventionally in Victorian times the kitchen was banished to the back of the house along with the servants, but at the Red House it was turned into a spacious room with windows opening out on to the garden. Elsewhere in the house Burne-Jones designed stained-glass windows and painted medieval scenes on the woodwork and walls; Rossetti painted settle door panels; Webb designed beds, tables, chairs and candlesticks, while

William Morris was a gifted and versatile artist, as adept at turning the image of the daisy (above) into a textile or wallpaper design ('Daisy', opposite) as he was a writer, furniture designer and illustrator. Even when it came to gardens, he 'knew all the ways and capabilities'.

Morris and Janey worked together to create embroidered hangings and paint floral patterns on the ceilings.

Unusually, the house plans included some detailed plantings for the garden: roses and jasmine planted where their evening scent would drift in through the dining room windows; a passion flower to climb up a wall and frame a pantry window. And the importance of the garden to Morris may be measured by the fact that he built his garden before he built his house.

Burne-Jones's wife, Georgiana, described the layout of the front garden as 'spaced formally into four little square gardens making a big square together, each of the smaller squares had a wattled fence round it with an opening by which one entered, and all over the fences roses grew thickly'. No planting plans survive for this cloistered, medieval-like garden, but Morris often expressed a fondness for sunflowers, hollyhocks and rose-covered trelliswork, and his sketchbooks from the Red House period include pages of drawings of curling leaves, climbing tendrils and trelliswork woven with plants, themes that were to be refined and repeated in his later designs. Perhaps the most potent hint of how the garden looked to Morris is revealed in a passage from his *The Story of the Unknown Church*: 'In the garden were trellises covered over with roses, and convolvulus, and the great-leafed fiery nasturtium; and specially all along by the poplar trees were the trellises, but on these grew nothing but deep crimson roses; the hollyhocks too were all out in blossom at that time, great spires of pink, and orange, and red, and white, with their soft downy leaves.'

William and Jane Morris left the Red House and its garden in 1865 and did not return. Life for both of them would never be the same again.

Morris wove leaf and flower motifs into designs such as 'Acanthus' (above) in a style that has remained popular for over a century. Yet the original inspiration for many of his designs sprang from the flower-filled borders at the Red House (right) which he had enjoyed for only six years.

KOBE

Isamu

Noguchi

(1904–1988)

Fifteen creamy smooth boulders are surrounded by the hypnotic contours of raked quartz. A single, precise gladiolus stands on a window ledge.

Weeds in the rice field
Cut and left lying just so –
Fertilizer!

goes a Japanese *haiku* attributed to the Zen master Basho, as if to demonstrate that the art of Zen gardening is the art of artlessness.

In the horticultural cross-fertilization between East and West, Japanese gardens were quick to make their mark in Europe and America. Aside from some strange pastiches filled with awkward boulders, fussy pagodas and bronze cranes, there have been several masterful creations: Tassa Eida's life-story garden at Tully in County Kildare, Ireland, the Clingendael in The Hague or the Nitobe Gardens in British Columbia, for example. When it came to the austere beauty of the Zen Buddhist garden, the Japanese-American artist Isamu Noguchi played an influential, but quite unpredictable, role in bringing the gardens of the East to the West.

Isamu Noguchi was a prolific artist who initially made a name for himself with his sensitive and perceptive portraiture: a chrome-plated bronze of his life-long friend, Buckminster Fuller; the bronze of another friend, Brooklyn-born composer George Gershwin; a tender portrait of his mother, made in spite of his insistence that he could never produce a good portrait of someone he knew too well.

Isamu Noguchi's works found their way into private and public collections across the world, but for the man who ended his years sculpting the land, the artist has been better remembered for works that were places rather than pieces. There is the sunken garden in the plaza outside the Chase Manhattan Bank in New York, his Jardin Japonais for the Unesco building in Paris and, the piece he most wanted to represent his life as an artist, the sanctuary-like Isamu Noguchi Garden Museum in New York. Imprisoned among the industrial buildings of Long Island City, Queens, near the 59th Street Bridge from Manhattan, the garden was one of the last works Isamu Noguchi produced before his death in December 1988.

Bare stones stand in a sand yard at Mure on the Japanese island of Shikoku (left). One of the many creations of the Japanese-American sculptor Isamu Noguchi, the garden served to bridge the divide between traditional and contemporary Japanese garden design.

Noguchi had purchased a group of factory buildings in Long Island City in the 1960s when he needed somewhere to store and construct his work. Like Barbara Hepworth and Henry Moore (see pages 154 and 16), Noguchi needed to create an exhibition space where his sculptures could be seen in the context of his workshops. Unlike these two artists, however, he had to build the garden from scratch. Planted with trees, shrubs and the artist's own sculptures, the garden was surrounded by the high walls of the buildings, their upper windows left unglazed so that the outdoor

breathed through into the indoor spaces. Part garden and part gallery, the site with its elemental materials – stone, wood, earth and air – resonated with the faint echoes of the ancestral Zen garden where, as Alan Watts wrote in *The Way of Zen*, 'the secret lies in balancing form with emptiness and, above all, in knowing when one has "said" enough.'

Noguchi described gardens as a sculpturing of space. His own sculptures, he said, were 'neither this nor that but a thing in space that affects our consciousness'. They formed 'what I call a garden, for want of a better name'. But whether he was laying down the bones of a garden or executing a brush drawing of the landscape, Isamu Noguchi was an artist with a deep-rooted identity crisis. In America, the Los Angeles-born artist was regarded as Japanese; in Japan, this son of a Japanese poet was seen as being too American for his own good. A garden encyclopedia will credit Noguchi as being a Japanese garden designer while a history of modern art describes him as an American-Japanese sculptor; and the man responsible for introducing the ubiquitous lampshade made of wire and unbleached rice paper into millions of homes earns himself yet another mention in the history of contemporary design. Isamu Noguchi was an enigma.

'I like to think of gardens as sculpturing of space,' Noguchi wrote. He took infinite care in arranging a courtyard of stones outside his studio in Japan (above) or in skilfully balancing the effect of trees and sculptures in his garden at Long Island City, New York (right).

In the early 1900s Noguchi's mother-to-be, an American writer, Leonie Gilmour, answered an advertisement placed in a newspaper by Yonejiro Noguchi. Noguchi was a Japanese poet living in America and he needed someone to help him translate his prose into English. The couple met and eventually were married, but by the time Isamu was born in 1904, Yonejiro had returned to Japan. Leonie Gilmour and Isamu followed him there and although they had a second child, Ailes, the relationship did not last. After an early education in Japan Isamu was sent to America at the age of fourteen to study at the progressive Interlaken School near Rolling Prairie in Indiana. He attended Columbia University briefly as a medical student, but when Leonie and Ailes returned to the States in 1920, he left to study sculpture at the Leonardo da Vinci School of Art in New York. Leonie Gilmour approved – she had always wanted her son to 'have eye and hand trained to express his ideas'.

Noguchi was brought up in America and Japan. His sculptural pieces (above and right) were influenced by Constantin Brancusi, his garden designs by the raked sand and rock gardens of Kyoto, creating 'a space in which art itself is so artless as to be totally unapparent'.

In 1927 Noguchi was awarded a Guggenheim Fellowship to travel and study and he promptly left for Paris to seek out the sculptor Constantin Brancusi, persuading the artist to take him on as a studio assistant. Brancusi, who had left his native Romania in 1904 and set off on foot for Paris, had been a student of Rodin's before he set up his own studio. Having concentrated on paring the elements of sculpture down to their essence, his graceful, highly polished pieces had already gained

Brancusi an international reputation when the twenty-three-year-old Noguchi arrived at his studio door.

After studying with Brancusi, Noguchi returned to the States to begin his portraiture in a studio in Carnegie Hall. But 1930 saw him restlessly journeying again, this time to Beijing on the Trans-Siberian railway where he would spend eight months studying brush drawing with a Chinese master and another seven months in Japan working in clay with a master potter. It was during this trip that Noguchi also rediscovered the traditions of the Zen gardens.

Throughout his life Isamu Noguchi worked and travelled, and travelled and worked. He designed stage sets for Martha Graham, costumes for the dancer Ruth Page, a fountain for the Ford Motor Company, a glass-plated coffee table, playground equipment, home interiors, stone slab sculptures and mixed media constructions. In the post-war years he visited the villagers of Gifu in Japan, renowned for their traditional lanterns made from the bark of mulberry trees. Once he had seen their work, Noguchi immediately began sketching plans for a wire-framed and rice paper lamp. Before long his Akari lights (*akari* means illumination through light) were in production and being copied worldwide.

He did not realize his first garden until the 1950s, although he had already made plans for several landscape environments and gardens. When the conflict between his two mother countries ended in blinding flashes of light over Nagasaki and Hiroshima with the dropping of America's atomic bomb, the artist proposed a garden for Hiroshima's Memorial of the Dead. The garden, he said, would represent 'a fence against the darkness', but it was turned down on the grounds that Noguchi was too American.

The rejection was a bitter blow for an artist who had become an ethnic casualty of the divergent cultures that characterized East and West. The arts establishment did not know what to do with the mercurial talents of an artist who had come under the eclectic influences of modern sculpture, Zen and traditional crafts such as calligraphy and gardening.

Noguchi had also experienced personal rejection: at one point he tried to re-establish a relationship with his father, by then remarried and with a new family, but instead of a happy reunion, he had to endure hours of what he called 'silent conversations' with the old man. In a final effort to anchor himself culturally, he took a Japanese wife, film star Shirley Yamaguchi, bought an old house in a rice valley near Kamakura and so thoroughly adopted archaic, traditional costumes and customs it startled his neighbours. Noguchi stopped doing portraiture and settled instead on working in clay and studying ancient Japanese crafts. Neither the home, the marriage nor this new ascetic way of life was to last and it was left to the world of corporate business to acknowledge his genius and provide him with the means to express it.

In 1956 the Bauhaus architect Marcel Breuer asked Noguchi to design a garden for the Unesco headquarters in Paris. Noguchi, firmly committed to the philosophy of the Zen garden, designed it in two parts: an upper terrace with carved boulders and square seats and a lower terrace filled with mounded plantings, pools and paved and grassy spaces. Stepping stones paced across the water and raked gravel surrounded some of the stones. This new Jardin Japonais relied on plants, rocks and even gardeners brought in from Japan and, while it rose from Noguchi's empathy for the Zen garden, the abstract, sculptural plantings and sharp, geometric arrangement of grass and stone stemmed, like Henry Moore's work (see page 16), from the animate, living forms of nature.

The traditional Zen garden was exemplified by the rock and sand gardens of Kyoto, and its most famous

Friend of George Gershwin and Buckminster Fuller, lover of Frida Kahlo, inventor of the ubiquitous wire and paper lantern, Isamu Noguchi created gardens that were just as challenging as his sculptures (left).

example at Ryoan-ji where, in the fifteenth century, five groups of rocks were laid out on a rectangle of raked sand, backed by a stone wall and surrounded by trees. Selecting the right rocks was an art in itself. *Bonseki* involved expeditions into the countryside to find stones perfectly shaped by weather and water. These were then stood for years where they would acquire natural colonies of mosses before being finally placed in the chosen garden. When in the early 1960s Noguchi was commissioned to design a garden for the Chase Manhattan Bank in New York he sent to Kyoto for his boulders and laid them on a bed of granite in a circular garden sunk into the plaza outside the bank. In winter the garden was dry, but in summer Noguchi set fountains into the garden which played water on to the stones.

Although the artist introduced trees and shrubs into his Long Island garden (above), several of Noguchi's environmental commissions lacked either soil or plants. 'It is my desire to view nature through nature's eyes and to ignore man as an object of veneration.'

Still in the 1960s, the IBM Corporation commissioned two gardens for their offices at Armonk, New York. Noguchi built the first with rough boulders set among trees and grass to represent the past. The second garden was designed to symbolize the future with a pyramid of Brazilian granite, a bronze sculpture based loosely on the DNA double helix molecule, a black concrete dome inscribed with formulae and an adjacent red concrete concave with a fountain set in it. And there were other public commissions: a fountain with a computerized flow of water at the Hart Plaza in

Detroit; the Marble Garden for the Beinecke Rare Book and Manuscript Library at Yale University in Connecticut; a Landscape of Time at the Federal Building in Seattle; and, finally, his own garden at Long Island City. Many of these later gardens lacked either soil or plants, Noguchi using instead his great sculptural forms to symbolize the forces of nature.

His thoroughly modern gardens were the product of a very twentieth-century artist – for fifty creative years Noguchi insisted that whether he was working on a stage set, a plaza, a table lamp or a garden, his work was always pure sculpture. To many people the gardens seemed to be far removed from the orthodoxy of the conventional garden bursting with growth and greenery. But for all their modernity, they have a resonance with the quiescent creations of the traditional Japanese gardens, whether it was the raked-sand and water gardens of the Zen Buddhists or some contemplative Tokyo garden planted with mounds of miniature evergreens and relentlessly clipped and pruned to preserve their shape and colour through all the seasons.

Noguchi's friend Buckminster Fuller once wrote: 'There is one outstandingly important fact regarding Spaceship Earth, and that is that no instruction book came with it.' In the absence of a proper manual, Isamu Noguchi offered instead a visionary way to look at it.

When the natural forms of the trees and shrubs in the garden assume their skeletal, winter shapes, Noguchi's elemental art suggests continuity through the seasons. He explained, 'The size and shape of each element is entirely relative to all the others and the given space.'

Patrick

Heron

(1920–1999)

In the mid 1920s the young Patrick Heron dutifully accompanied his parents on a visit to the Cornish country home of a family friend, William Arnold-Forster. While the two families discussed the topics of the day, the child wandered off into the garden with his pencil and sketch pad. The garden was a child's wonderland. Surrounded by Cornish moorland, the house, romantically named Eagles Nest, stood perched on a hill 600 ft (200 m) above the rolling blue Atlantic. Corncrakes called from the fields below and buzzards hung in the air, looking down on the towering tors which topped the neighbouring hills. Several of these lumps of silvered granite, poised one on top of another like some giant infant's pebble pile, stood in the garden of Eagles Nest, one great boulder being so finely balanced on the rock beneath that the child could set it rocking with his own small hands.

The drawings from those early days – 'I had already decided at the age of five that I wanted to be a painter,' the artist would recall – were testimony to a precious talent. Over seventy years later, on the century's turn, Patrick Heron had become one of Britain's leading abstract artists. He was also now in permanent residence at Eagles Nest. During the intervening years he had grown up, moved away and married and, although he and his wife Delia made regular forays back to Cornwall, the couple had settled to live and work in London. Then, in the 1950s, Eagles Nest fell vacant. Patrick and Delia Heron moved in.

There was little to see of Eagles Nest from the serpentine coast road which headed west out of St Ives. Apart from the glimpse of a house gable framed by an avenue of stunted sycamores and pale blue hydrangeas,

Patrick Heron, one of the most important painters of his generation, had been entranced as a child by this Cornish garden with its massive boulders (left). A quarter of a century later, fate was to draw him back.

the garden lay hidden behind its hedges of escallonia and its traditional stone and sod walls. Even from within, the tall hedges and a maze-like network of paths obscured the shape and plan of the labyrinthine garden. In the 1980s, when Patrick Heron joined a television crew filming Eagles Nest from a helicopter, he was given a buzzard's eye view of his home. Seen from above, the house and drive were flanked by a garden on either side, each grouped around its own granite tor, with a third garden tumbling down among more boulders at the front of the house. Each of the three gardens was subdivided into garden rooms – shrubberies, kitchen gardens, an orchard, a nursery bed, a terraced lawn, a fernery – while the grass and gravel paths, which wound their way through these rooms, threaded the gardens together like a necklace around the throat of the house.

The path at the front of the house wound between a pack of rocks, dipped down into a shade garden and then ascended a precipitous wooden step ladder back to the house. To the east, a second path slipped between granite walls, circled a prominent tor and wound its way back to the house through a kitchen garden, a little ash grove and a scented garden. The path to the west led past a second kitchen garden, twisted around another great granite monolith, travelled

down avenues crowded with camellias and azaleas and finally emerged on a sunken green terrace which looked out over the sea.

Many celebrated people have stood shielding their eyes against the ocean's glare and breathing in the view from this terrace: Virgina Woolf, the surrealist Roland Penrose and his wife, the *Vogue* photographer Lee Miller (friend of Picasso and Man Ray), Barbara Hepworth and Ben Nicholson among them. D. H. Lawrence once walked the clifftops below during breaks between writing *Women In Love*. Even Gertrude Jekyll (see page 170) lived for a while in the cottage next door, leaving behind one of her trademarks, a neat, hand-built wall of sparkling granite to protect its garden.

More recent visitors learned to look for the unexpected at every turn of a path: a white wisteria clinging to the lichened lea of a boulder; the glancing scent of a winter viburnum; a cloud of pink nerines grown in upturned rhubarb forcing pots; pockets of crimson cyclamen flowering at the feet of azaleas and New Zealand hoherias. In winter the garden glowed with green, trailing lichens, silky black and grey liverworts and the soft pads of moss which patterned every branch and unturned stone. In spring and summer each garden room burst into bloom: a billowing mass of feathery foliage and yellow flower on a glasshouse mimosa, the broad, fragrant white heads of an olearia, the scarlet efflorescence of a 'Gloire de Nantes' camellia. The rush of colours seemed to echo what one critic called the 'exhilarating rashness and brevity' of Patrick Heron's own painting.

Patrick Heron was born at Headingley in Leeds in 1920, but his family moved to Cornwall when the artist was five. When he was seven, the family stayed for five winter months at Eagles Nest: 'I remember it vividly,' recalled Heron: 'today's thirty-foot-high eucryphia were then just two-foot, rounded clumps. I drew them all the time.' But in 1929 his father's business, the textiles company Cresta Silks, took them away from the Cornish moors and eastwards into the suburbs of Welwyn Garden City in Hertfordshire. Ten years later, as the young Patrick Heron started to study

'Painting as such is abstract. Yet the power of that abstraction is its capacity to render the outside world visible,' wrote Heron in 1987. His '12–30 March: 1994' illustrates his point.

*The white flower heads of libertia, the skeletal forms of New Zealand flax (*Phormium*) and wind-tolerant senecios pattern the edge of the sunken green terrace at Eagles Nest (opposite).*

The fragrant Camellia sasanqua, *which seldom survives outdoors in Britain, blooms in the lea of one of the many granite boulders that punctuate the craggy garden at Eagles Nest (left).*

'Green and Mauve Horizontals: January 1958' (right) was among the canvases that helped establish Patrick Heron as one of the most exciting painters of the second half of the twentieth century.

at the Slade School of Fine Art in London, war broke out. Heron, a committed pacifist, became a farm labourer, hoeing and harvesting root crops on the windswept wastes of the East Anglian fens. He fell ill several times and eventually he was sent to Cornwall to work alongside one of Britain's most creative potters, Bernard Leach. When the war was over, Heron met and married Delia Reiss and, as he began to paint again, the couple moved to London. For the next eleven years Heron not only painted (his portraits of T. S. Eliot and Herbert Read now hang in the National Portrait Gallery in London), but also worked as an art critic for magazines such as the *New Statesman*, and as a teacher at the Central School of Arts and Crafts.

Influenced by artists such as Henri Matisse and Pierre Bonnard, Heron's paintings reflected a lust for light and colour. He developed a progressively abstract style and by the mid 1950s he was seen as one of the most original artists of his generation. He exhibited in London, New York, Switzerland and Australia, lectured in the United States, Australia and Japan, and worked as artist-in-residence and visiting artist in New South Wales and New Zealand; he designed textiles, stained-glass windows and a site-specific outdoor installation: 'Big Painting Sculpture' for Stag Place in London. As he experimented with the juxtaposition of colour and the interaction and interpretation of form, people repeatedly asked him about the connection between his 'rock-and-boulder-littered spur of the moors' and his paintings. 'The question baffled me,' he confessed – Heron was unaware of any link between his two passions, his landscape and his pictures: 'There had never been a single overt, direct connection or relationship or conscious derivation of any sort between the two.'

Laid down by Arnold-Forster, himself a Slade-trained painter, the garden at Eagles Nest arose as a

A grey slate garden table stands sheltered by a windbreak of escallonia (left), the shape of the clipped bush echoing the weather-hewn, rounded form of the garden boulders. 'I'm not a gardener,' insisted Patrick Heron. 'My contribution has been to shape the garden.'

sensible response to its wild location. Set so high above the shore, the garden regularly bore the full force of the salt-laden winds that swept in from the sea ('during our first winter here Delia and I used to lie in bed wondering if the roof would blow away') and Arnold-Forster's first task had been to protect the site with walls, hedges and shelter belts. He adopted the age-old Cornish solution of earthen walls lined with stones and topped with turfs, and planted hedges of escallonia, a plant adept at withstanding wind and sea spray. Having created protected pockets within the garden, he could begin to take advantage of the temperate climate, the neutral to acid soil and the clear light: the Cornish coast retained its pellucid light even when ocean mists rolled in or the sky and sea turned battleship grey. ('On this peninsula,' explained Heron, 'the ocean acts like a great mirror reflecting light up into a humid atmosphere which reflects it back across the land.')

'Fourteen Discs: July 20 1963' (above). Heron's works are resolutely non-figurative and a joyous celebration of colour. He once wrote: 'The only rule I follow while painting is this: I always allow my hand to surprise me.'

Arnold-Forster planted his tolerant senecios and heathers, hardy camellias and azaleas, robust New Zealand satin flowers (*Libertia grandiflora*) and crocosmia. Since he was also researching material for his book *Shrubs for the Milder Counties*, he experimented with less tolerant plants such as banksia, eucryphia and *Metrosideros lucida*, a scarlet-flowered relation of the myrtle.

When Patrick and Delia Heron moved to Eagles Nest in 1956 they experienced the occasional disaster: 'We lost the *Metrosideros lucida*, one of only about four in England, in one bad frost. I had seen it in bloom on the east coast of New Zealand, like a stripe of paint across the landscape. We managed to find a

Childe

Hassam

(1859-1935)

The one flower painted more often than any other by the Impressionists was the poppy. It was a characteristic and iridescent presence in the work of Renoir, Monet, Mary Cassatt and Van Gogh. For Frederick Childe Hassam, too, the red poppy became an important and recurring motif. It appeared in a series of paintings that have been thought of as the most beautiful of his entire output.

Hassam was one of the major figures of the Impressionist movement in America. A restless, itinerant individual, he was always on the move and always painting – it was an activity he enjoyed more than any other, which accounts for his prolific output of some several thousand works in watercolour, oil, pastels and printmaking media. Hassam used a palette of vibrant, high-key colours: gold, amber, red, with emerald greens and blues, a palette with which he confidently created an especial quality of sunlight. Hassam's trademark was the brightness of his colour. If critics complained that his canvases were too intensely blue, he would answer unapologetically that he preferred 'air that is breathable'.

Childe Hassam was an astute artist who combined self-promotion with flair and determination. He achieved recognition early on in his life, became a popular artist and remains so to this day. Part of that recognition was due to the hospitality and vision of his friend Celia Thaxter. Her clapboard summer retreat on Appledore Island, part of the Isles of Shoals off the coast of Maine, New England, stood in a region of exceptional natural beauty and for over two decades Hassam came to stay and paint her flower garden. Appledore Island, with its rough ocean water, white rocky outcrops and spectacular sunsets, was a formidable site for a flower garden, but Thaxter, a poet, essayist and gardener, enjoyed the challenge of creating her cutting garden and of cultivating flowers in the rocky island soil. She succeeded to the extent that, at the height of the season, her garden would produce more than a hundred freshly cut bouquets of flowers a week.

The figure of Childe Hassam (above) is less familiar today than at the turn of the twentieth century, when he was regarded as one of the leading figures in the American Impressionist movement. One of his principal inspirations was the simple poppy blooms (left) in the New Hampshire garden of his friend, the poet Celia Thaxter.

Among Childe Hassam's strongest and most atmospheric works were twenty-two watercolours that he created specifically as illustrations and headpieces for Celia Thaxter's *An Island Garden,* a book she published in 1894. In it she detailed the broad range of flowers that were cultivated, explained the reasons for her preferences and choices and punctuated her account with hints and tips for successful gardening. Celia loved poppies and she devoted a complete chapter of this book to them. She grew a number of varieties and was passionate about the richness of their colour, enthusing about the different shades of yellow gold eschscholzias, the California poppies, about the

resonance and subtleties of rose, scarlet, crimson and lilac Shirley poppies whose saucer-shaped blooms grew to as much as 4 in (10 cm) across. She loved, too, the bright yellows, oranges and whites of the Iceland poppies and the dazzling intensity of the large Oriental poppy.

She grew her poppies in eleven rectangular raised flower beds, the earth held in place by wooden planking set on edge like the sides of a box. The entire plot was enclosed by fencing made of the same white boarding, which made the clapboard house as much an extension of the garden as the garden was an extension

The raised beds of Celia Thaxter's cutting garden (right) on Appledore Island, off the coast of Maine, were capable of producing hundreds of fresh bouquets of flowers all through the summer. For twenty summers Hassam came here to paint watercolours such as 'Poppies' (above).

of the house. Over fifty different varieties of flowering plants spilled in a profusion of blooms out of this highly organized and well-planned plot, roses, clematis, dahlias, wisteria, phlox, asters, delphiniums and blue cornflowers among them. Early each morning at five o'clock, while the rest of the household was asleep, Celia would go out into her garden, to experience on her own what she described as 'a silent joy that fills me with infinite content'.

Her friend Childe Hassam was born into a long-established and prosperous New England family in Dorchester, Massachusetts, the son of a merchant who collected antiques. Early on in his life he decided against a college education, preferring to study art, and went to work in the office of a Boston wood engraver where he produced illustrations, letterheads and ornamental designs. In 1883 he travelled to Europe, visiting Italy, Spain, the Low Countries and England and, on his return to Boston, he made the most of these travels by exhibiting numerous paintings from the trip. For the next three years he studied art seriously until he found work as a freelance magazine and newspaper illustrator.

He made a second trip to Europe in 1886 to extend his technical range and enrolled at the Académie Julian in Paris, a school that was a stimulation and a starting point for so many American artists. Here he discovered Impressionism and, though still abroad, held a number of exhibitions, again in Boston, in one of which he showed mainly views of gardens and streets in Paris and its suburbs. His work earned him increasing recognition on both sides of the Atlantic and, in the Paris Salon of 1888, he was awarded the Gold Medal Prize for his canvas 'Grand Prix Day'.

For American artists in France, the year of the Paris World Fair in 1889 (an occasion landmarked by the sensation of Eiffel's tower) was a very good year. Prizes were awarded to a number of them, including Childe Hassam, who returned to America that autumn with a Bronze Medal. The following year Hassam began to work in a more developed and Impressionistic manner, a technique much like Claude Monet's pointillist style, using dotted brushstrokes that gave a broken, vibrant and luminous effect. Within twelve months he had become significantly accomplished in his handling of the technique. Although a number of other American artists were also working in this way, Childe Hassam seemed to come closest to Monet's approach. He, however, never publicly acknowledged the depth of Monet's influence and, since he was essentially self-taught, he remained always reticent about his artistic background.

In December 1897 Hassam resigned from the Society of American Artists, disenchanted both with the overwhelming quantity and mediocre quality of the works

the Society exhibited. Like-minded painters from New York and Boston vowed to break away from the Society and establish a new group of their own, sympathetic to the then new directions in art, principally Impressionism. They formed the group of The Ten American Painters, or The Ten as they became known, and for the next twenty years they were to exhibit together.

After his return to America in 1889 Hassam based himself in New York, but he would stay in the city

A gull scrutinizes the delphiniums and poppies in Celia Thaxter's Atlantic garden (left). A pupil of his watercolour classes in Boston, Thaxter invited Hassam to visit her garden one summer in 1890; he returned here every year, even after the poet's death. Her garden has been maintained with her original layout (above).

only in the winter, working on his studio pieces and urban scenes – he was fascinated by the movement of figures and the bustle of metropolitan life. During the summer, however, Hassam would paint in the coastal resorts of New York state and New England. Since he loved the coastal light and landscapes and never stopped painting them, this was a pattern he would follow for the rest of his life, but from 1890 onwards Appledore Island became his favourite summer haunt. For the next twenty-two years, even after Celia Thaxter's death in 1894, Hassam returned to her white clapboard house to paint its summer garden.

He had met Thaxter when she had been a pupil in his watercolour classes back in Boston, and when she invited him to Appledore Island, it marked the beginning of a long-lasting friendship. Her summer retreat on the island attracted the cultural élite of Boston and became a kind of informal salon where visitors engaged with musicians, literary figures and other artists, but for Hassam and Thaxter it also offered the solitude and quiet focus they both needed for their work. He celebrated her garden in paint, she commemorated it in poetry and prose.

In 'Thaxter's Garden', 1892 (above), Hassam used his Impressionist skills to catch the colour and flow of the flowers and to highlight the sun on the white clapboard house. Heliopsis and cosmos weave among timber railings (right), bringing high-summer colour to the garden.

Thaxter, who had great faith in Hassam's work, was both host, visionary and, through her garden cultivation, influence. It was she who advised Hassam to put aside his first name, Frederick, and to make the most of his romantic-sounding middle name, Childe.

She also pointed his painter's eye towards particular scenes and flowers. The water lily held a singular place in the history of Impressionist painting and although Childe Hassam had never visited Monet's studio at Giverny where the *maître* painted his nymphaea outside in their lily ponds (see page 134), Hassam found himself painting water lilies in the parlour when Celia Thaxter brought them into the house and, treating them like other cut flowers, set them up in long, fluted, narrow vases for still life painting. And although Thaxter's beloved poppies would last little longer than a day as cut flowers, she would treat them as she treated her lilies, and Hassam made a number of paintings of her flower arrangements in the study at Appledore, where red corn poppies were mixed with the orange and yellow of Iceland poppies. Candace Wheeler, in her 1901 publication *Content in a Garden*, acknowledged Celia Thaxter's creative flair: 'I have never seen such realized possibilities of colour. The fine harmonic sense of this woman and artist and poet thrilled through these long chords of colour, and filled the room with an atmosphere which made it like living in a rainbow.'

Hassam, too, understood many of the mysteries of colour. He knew how to enhance the intensity of one colour by using it in conjunction with its opposite, complementary colour – for example, by rendering even more vividly the blazing intensity of a red poppy flower by setting it against its complementary green foliage.

Thaxter's garden gave him the opportunity to realize this knowledge on canvas in works such as 'The Garden in its Glory', painted in 1892. In the picture, Hassam placed the metal archway, which led from the cutting garden to the front porch of the clapboard house, in the centre of his canvas. Saturated in lush

greenery, the archway was pinpointed with the glowing reds of poppies and hollyhocks (a flower particularly tolerant of this coastal location) and made redder by the green foliage. He added to this composition the massed bright yellows of coreopsis around the steps of the porch and portrayed the density of all the flowers and foliage with rapid, angular brushstrokes moved in all directions. Reviewing one of Hassam's exhibitions of watercolours, one critic declared that his paintings would 'give the world which cannot get to Appledore Island an idea of the particular wealth of colour which the marine atmosphere lends to the poppies and marigolds which grow in the poet's garden.'

When he painted this garden, in addition to the light and the saturation of colour Hassam responded to the breadth and exposure of the site and to its cliff top position which looked out over the Atlantic Ocean. Although the actual size of Celia Thaxter's little plot was only some 50 ft (15 m) long and 15 ft (5 m) wide, Hassam's canvases gave a sense of flowers growing in an unfettered space. Painting and sketching in the context of the land and the sea and the sky, the artist produced works with a threefold unity that combined the flower pieces with landscape and seascape.

Although after her death Celia Thaxter's clapboard house was destroyed by fire, the garden has risen again and been restored according to her original layout. In a sense, however, the words of Celia Thaxter and the Impressionist colours of Childe Hassam had already ensured that this little island garden would be preserved for ever in a unique confluence of poetry and painting.

Childe Hassam was a painter of the nineteenth century, an artist in tune with the temperament of his time. His death in 1935 was to signal the end of Impressionist painting in America.

The little garden on Appledore Island brought together and inspired both poet and painter. Although the artists have left long ago, coreopsis and centaurea and many other flowers still unfailingly appear each year.

Peter Paul

Rubens

(1577–1640)

Christmas 1630 proved to be a turning point for the Flemish master, Peter Paul Rubens. He had decided to quit politics, having recently returned from a series of unsuccessful diplomatic missions in London, Paris and Brussels. With enough commissions to keep him busy for what were to be his final ten years, he was enjoying the benefits of a growing reputation. And three weeks before Christmas he and his teenage bride, Hélène Fourment, had married. Rubens was fifty-three, Hélène was the same age as the elder of his two sons, sixteen-year-old Albert. She was to bear him four children and, it seems, make him a happy man.

Hard-working and industrious, Rubens led a well-regulated life. He would rise early and, after attending Mass, return to his studio. As he prepared his brushes, he would listen to his paid reader recite from his favourite Latin authors. Following a light lunch, Rubens would work through until late afternoon when, after a stroll in the garden with Hélène, he would take to the saddle for a little exercise. At the end of the day he frequently dined with friends and discussed the issues of the day – the state of his health (he suffered badly from gout), the astronomical price of tulip bulbs, the demands of his patrons – before retiring to his home.

The Rubenshuis and its garden, faithfully restored with period materials in 1946, stands on the Wapper in the centre of Antwerp. In the sixteenth century this was the richest city in northern Europe and its parks, gardens and civic architecture reflected the well-to-do lives of affluent Flemish burghers. Rubens' own little Baroque mansion, which he had purchased after marrying his first wife, Isabella Brant, was a measure of the artist's standing in an affluent society. The ornate façade of the Rubenshuis was decorated with the busts of classical philosophers and frescoes that represented the lives of the gods. Inside the house there was a modest suite of living rooms and bedrooms and a semi-circular gallery which the artist used, not to exhibit his own works, but to display his precious collection of antiquities, traded with the English Duke of Buckingham for several paintings, and his collection of Flemish and Italian paintings. Rubens' studio lay parallel to the house and, spacious though it was, could accommodate the work of no more than three projects at any one time. When the room was filled with the bustle of a busy painter's workshop, he could seek sanctuary in the large quadrangular courtyard and flower garden that stood between the studio and the house.

*The shrewd eyes of Peter Paul Rubens gaze out from his self-portrait (above). In 1630 the fifty-three-year-old painter married a teenage bride and settled at the Rubenshuis in Antwerp (left). Now open to the public, its seventeenth-century garden grows foxgloves, rue, monkshood (*Aconitum*) and rose campion (*Lychnis coronaria*).*

By 1621 the artist had altered the building and its grounds to suit his particular purposes and built an elaborate Baroque portico to link the house to the

CARIOR EST ILLIS HOMO QUAM SIBI
SATYRA X

studio and to form a picturesque approach to the courtyard and garden. With its three wide arches framing the garden beyond, the portico was probably designed by Rubens himself; he was certainly delighted by its appearance and he often painted the portico and garden into many of his later works. The garden, subdivided into four rectangular parterres and surrounded by low, clipped hedges, was neat and symmetrical and planted with the popular plants of the day which, by 1630, may well have included the country's most popular bulb, the tulip. From 1630 on, Rubens' work increasingly reflected his more settled way of life as he reaped the rewards of his extraordinary past as a scholar, linguist, diplomat and painter.

Peter Paul Rubens believed he had been born in Cologne in 1577. His parents, Jan and Maria, apparently did not reveal to their son that, due to an unfortunate indiscretion by his father, a lawyer and respected alderman, their son had been born in the little Westphalian town of Siegen. Having fled from political troubles in Antwerp, the Rubens family had settled in Cologne where Jan Rubens became a legal adviser to Anne of Saxony, the wife of the Prince of Orange. But when his professional relationship become a scandalously intimate one, Jan Rubens was thrown into jail and only saved from a sentence of death by the intercession of his wife. The family was banished to Siegen where Maria bore two children; Peter Paul was her younger son. When Rubens' father died the family finally returned to Antwerp, a city which had survived its political upheavals and was now entering a new period of relative peace and stability.

Rubens attended the local grammar school where, under the direction of his classics headmaster, he learned to read, write and love the classics. Antwerp was a city which approved of its artists and Rubens seems to have experienced no difficulty studying to become one; by the age of twenty-one, he had qualified as a technically proficient artist.

A scholar, linguist and diplomat as well as a painter, Rubens may also have designed the magnificent Baroque portico (left) that linked his house and studio and which was to feature in many of his paintings.

Two years later Rubens made a inspirational move and travelled to Italy. He became court painter at the palace of the Duke of Mantua alongside such luminaries as the composer Claudio Monteverdi and the scientist and astronomer Galileo. He was exposed to the riches of the Italian culture, to its houses, its gardens and its art, and especially the work of Titian, whom Rubens credited with giving painting 'its perfume'. As he copied the works of Titian and the other great Venetian masters, in order to understand their technique and to sharpen his own, this highly literate and, by all accounts, extremely affable young painter caught the eye of his patron, the Duke. Rubens, who was fluent not only in Flemish and Italian, but in French and Latin, was considered sufficiently trustworthy to be dispatched on diplomatic missions to Rome and later to Madrid. Wherever the painter went, he invariably impressed his hosts; when he visited the Spanish court, bringing several paintings as presents for the king, Philip III, the works were damaged during the journey. Rubens promptly, and expertly, repainted the damaged works and immediately earned himself several new commissions from the king.

In 1608, when Rubens learned of his mother's deteriorating health, he travelled back to Antwerp. She died before he could reach home and, although he had planned to return to Italy, he changed his mind and stayed in Antwerp. At the age of thirty-one, Rubens the artist had come of age. He accepted the position of court painter to the Spanish governors of the Netherlands, an appointment he would hold until his death, and for the next thirty-two years concentrated on the body of work which would make him one of the most important artists in northern Europe.

Among the cornucopia of flowers in this portrayal of Flora and Zephyr (right) are snowdrops, celandines, primulas, harebells, honeysuckle, lilies, irises, carnations, fritillaries and, prominently featured, the exotic tulip. This newly introduced bloom (above) had caught the imagination of, it seemed, everyone in the land, and Rubens was no exception.

In 1609 he married Isabella Brant, the daughter of his great friend Johannes Brant and a woman who, he maintained, 'had none of the failings common to her sex'. He set up a studio in his father-in-law's house and began work on his many commissions. When Isabella died in 1626, the painter was heart-broken and left Antwerp on several more diplomatic missions to France, Spain and England, in each country triumphing as a painter if not always as a politician. More honours and courtly commissions followed. In Madrid he befriended the young painter Diego Velázquez and coped with the competition at court for the honour of posing for the master; Charles I of England knighted him and commissioned him to do a series of paintings for the ceiling of the banqueting hall at Whitehall Palace; in France his series of paintings for the Luxembourg Palace was credited with changing the course of that nation's painting. '*Le Dieu est là*' – God is here – wrote one commentator.

Rubens' affair with Italy brought light to his paintings and inspiration to his home life. In 1616, ten years before Isabella's death, he had begun work on the house at Wapper. Five years later he had succeeded in turning it into his interpretation of an Italian *palazzo* – during a stay in Genoa, the artist had fallen for the genteel little Genoese palaces with their stucco and mural decorations, their terraces, loggias and gardens filled with sculptures, urns, fountains and tub-grown plants.

When he founded his workshop at Wapper he modelled it on the Italian pattern where the 'master' created while his student painters and apprentices assiduously copied. When he undertook a commission Rubens would execute rapid ink and wash sketches, adding detailed instructions concerning colour and light. The customer would be shown an oil sketch based on the preliminary sketches together with some stock anatomical studies, usually in chalk, from the Rubens studio. Once the commission was approved Rubens and his students would complete the work, the degree of his involvement depending on the value of the commission.

Such was the master's control over his apprentices that it was impossible to distinguish one hand from another in some of the paintings.

Similarly, when Rubens came to lay out and plant his garden, the artist may have sketched his ideas and instructed others to do the work. Although in most of sixteenth-century Antwerp an ornamental garden was considered less important than the practical herb and kitchen garden, there was a fashion, set by the Court in Brussels, for symmetrical, enclosed gardens with little bowers and arbours. But by the end of the century, and later when the first clods of earth were being turned at the Rubenshuis, the Mediterranean winds of change were blowing through the neat and ordered Flemish gardens. Following the Italian fashion, ornamental gardens, designed to be viewed as status symbols, were being linked to the architecture of the house, rather than being treated as a separate element. The flatlands of Antwerp prohibited the use of the Italianate terrace, but intricate geometric shapes, arbours grown to form open-sided arcades or loggias, topiaried shrubs and trickling fountains were enthusiastically adopted. There was equal enthusiasm for introducing new foreign plants such as the lilac and, of course, the famous tulip.

Here, in 'Garden of Love' (above), as the painter toys with the medieval concept of the garden as a symbol of love and fertility, Rubens worked in elements of his own very fashionable garden (right) with its clipped yew hedges and container-grown citrus trees.

Rubens had begun his final body of work in 1630, a period when he drew heavily on his domestic life, his house, his garden and his young wife. Among the many affectionate portraits was 'Rubens and Hélène Fourment Walking With Their Child', in which he pictured the family strolling through a garden towards his own

Baroque portico with, in the background, a stand of irises and tulips. The date was 1633; in 1634 tulip mania struck the country.

A European ambassador travelling in Turkey a century earlier had noticed a profusion of cup-shaped flowers growing in a Turkish garden. He collected specimens of what the Turks called the *lalé* to take home to Vienna, but in a confusing exchange with his guide, the ambassador came away with the name 'tulip' – the guide had been likening the shape of the *lalé* to his turban or *tulipand*. The name, and the mania, for this distinctive bloom was born. The eminent Flemish botanist Charles de L'Ecluse, *le père de tous les beaux jardins* – the father of all beautiful gardens – according to one admirer, had been successfully introducing exotic bulbs and tubers, including elegant crown imperial fritillaries and narcissi, and dainty anemones and hyacinths, to the gardens of northern Europe. He procured tulip bulbs from the Viennese ambassador and, as he grew them on, noted the tulip's habit of breaking into variegated forms from a single colour. When he published his findings he not only helped lay the foundations for the modern Dutch bulb industry, but also brought this singularly beautiful flower to the attention of the north European gardeners. For four years the variegated forms caused a flurry of interest: fortunes were staked on single specimens (and whole families ruined by rash speculation) and the stately, nodding heads of the misnamed *lalé* found a place both in Rubens' garden and in his paintings.

Like Renoir, Rubens' hands were crippled during his final years, and while his gout affected his brushstrokes, he continued to paint, producing an almost impressionistic effect in some of his last works. When he died in 1640, the diplomat, scholar, linguist and painter left the world, and his tulip-filled garden, a fulfilled man. He had been, said a friend, 'born to please and delight in all he does'.

Rubens, Antwerp's most famous son, is commemorated throughout the city. In the Nachtegalenpark is a garden, the Hortens Rubensiana, devoted to his memory.

Paul

Cézanne

(1839–1906)

At the turn of the twentieth century the painter Paul Cézanne worked tirelessly from his studio and garden on the Chemin des Lauves in Aix-en-Provence in southern France. Every morning, the sixty-year-old painter with his white beard and penetrating stare would leave the house dressed in his dark, shabby three-piece suit, a small easel under one arm, a canvas tucked under the other. He might pause on the short flight of stone steps, hewn from rough Provençal stone, that led down to the white gravel terrace of the garden. Behind him a fig tree and a frenzy of climbing plants surrounded the front door and reached up to the raw sienna shutters and pale blue windows of the house; before him, in a motley array of terracotta pots and stone troughs, spider plants (*Chlorophytum comosum*), silver-spiked fountain grass and scented pelargoniums grew in profusion in the dappled shade of an old Judas tree (*Cercis siliquastrum*).

Cézanne would set off for the surrounding countryside where he would paint until the midday heat and hazy air forced him to return. While the local Provençal people closed their shutters and took *la sieste* Cézanne would sit on his terrace and continue to paint in the shade, working on watercolour or oil sketches to create his intimate garden studies – a pelargonium in its terracotta pot, or the intricate patterns of the overlapping leaves that climbed the outside wall of the studio. In complete contrast to his oil paintings, which usually took him months to complete, these brief sketches were remarkable for the lightness of their touch. Later in the afternoon, as the temperature fell and the light regained its clarity, Cézanne would return to his favourite landscape subjects until, finally, the approaching darkness drove the artist home.

When Paul Cézanne painted his self-portrait (above), between 1877 and 1880, he was still struggling to make his name in Paris. Over twenty years later, when the art world had finally recognized his genius, he had retreated to the seclusion of his home in his native Provence (left).

A self-taught artist, Paul Cézanne produced paintings from his Provençal seclusion that would eventually change the course of twentieth-century art. He prepared the way for new artistic movements such as Cubism with Pablo Picasso and Georges Braque, and Fauvism with Henri Matisse, but what inspired Cézanne, like so many artists before and since, was his garden and the natural world which lay within it. ‘Art must make Nature eternal in our imagination,’ he once wrote. ‘What lies behind Nature? Nothing perhaps. Perhaps everything.’ Cézanne was deeply attached to his native Provence, with its rocky hills and vineyards, its rugged holm and cork oaks, its cypress groves and olive trees. For Cézanne the burnished landscape was resilient, solid, resistant to change; every leaf, every tree and every hill was sharply defined by the crystal clear light of the morning and the scenery under the deep blue sky

than a lawyer. With his father's grudging blessing and a small allowance, Cézanne left to study life drawing in Paris.

Although he had managed to reach the city of his dreams and was reunited with his old friend Zola, Cézanne suffered a series of setbacks. L'Ecole des Beaux-Arts refused him a student place and the Paris Salon rejected his paintings for their annual exhibition. With his thick Provençal accent and in his dishevelled clothes, the young provincial painter was regarded as a rustic eccentric and made unwelcome in Parisian circles. Despondent, Cézanne returned to Aix for a fruitless year working in his father's bank before making his way back to Paris to enrol in life drawing classes.

seemed to be soaked in colour. 'Objects are silhouetted not only in black and white, but also in blue, red, brown and violet,' Cézanne noted.

In his youth, however, Cézanne did not appreciate the significance of his Provençal inheritance. His ambition was to be immersed in the art world of cosmopolitan Paris.

He had been born in Aix-en-Provence in 1839, the eldest of the three children of a prosperous businessman. When Cézanne attended college in 1852 he struck up a friendship with the French novelist Emile Zola, took up the cause of art and literature, and wrote poetry during idyllic sojourns swimming and fishing on the river. This carefree period later provided the painter with the inspiration for his famous 'Bathers' series. In 1859, Cézanne, despite his developing passion for the arts, was sent to study law and for two unhappy years he neglected his course work and filled his law books with pencil sketches and verses until, eventually, he convinced his father that he would make a better artist

'Nature causes me the greatest of difficulties,' Cézanne confessed to his college friend, the novelist Emile Zola. He struggled for weeks on a single painting such as 'Maisons et Arbres' (above), yet despite his diligence, success as an artist continued to elude him.

Gradually he began to meet the emerging Impressionist artists such as Claude Monet, Pierre-Auguste Renoir, Camille Pissarro and Alfred Sisley, men who would change his life. Not that his life was uneventful: one of the women who modelled at his life class was a young book-keeper, Hortense Fiquet. Hortense did not share Cézanne's enthusiasm for painting although she did agree to model for a number of his portraits. Since Cézanne was a meticulous and methodical worker who demanded that his sitter remain motionless for long periods, the sessions were long and tedious. Nevertheless Cézanne and Fiquet became lovers and had a son, Paul, on whom Cézanne doted. Fearing his father's disapproval, Cézanne kept his life with Hortense and his son Paul a secret from his own family for eight years; his fears were not unfounded, for when rumours of the liaison finally reached his father in Aix-en-Provence, Cézanne's father promptly halved his allowance.

The artist, whose paintings would one day change hands for inconceivable sums of money, was still receiving a derisive response to his work. The ground-breaking Impressionist exhibition of 1874 to which Cézanne contributed was roundly condemned by

the critics, one of them remarking that the paintings appeared to have been created by 'firing bullets of paint at the canvas'. Edouard Manet, one of the fathers of Impressionism and a painter who previously had praised Cézanne's still lifes, now described him as like 'a brick-layer laying on paint with a trowel'. Cézanne grew increasingly embittered by his lack of recognition and the mockery of his friends. When Zola depicted him as a washed-up old painter in his novel *L'Oeuvre*, Cézanne finished their friendship.

Obstinately, the artist carried on, encouraged at least by Pissarro. Nine years his senior, Pissarro instructed Cézanne to work hard, use pure colours and trust his instincts: 'Do not be shy of Nature! You must be bold, even at the risk of going wrong and making mistakes. There is only one teacher: Nature,' Pissarro told Cézanne as they worked side by side, painting in the open air. Gradually, as his style matured, Cézanne's confidence grew. He returned to Provence to paint the landscape and wrote to Pissarro enthusing about his rediscovered affinity for the region. When Pissarro saw Cézanne's work from this period, he was taken aback by the achievements of his hard-working student, predicting that Cézanne 'might surprise the art world yet'.

Cézanne's fortunes finally improved in 1886 when, in August, his father died, leaving the forty-seven-year-old painter a considerable sum of money. 'The man was a genius,' said Cézanne: 'he left me with an income of 25,000 francs.' Financially secure at last, Cézanne abandoned Paris altogether and set to work in a studio

After the death of his father, Cézanne abandoned the Parisian art scene, set up his studio at Jas de Bouffan (above), with its plane trees and irises, and withdrew into his work. 'I do nothing which I have not seen, and what I paint exists,' he insisted in the face of criticism.

at the family home in Jas de Bouffan in Aix, producing some of his most famous paintings, including 'The Card Players'. Collectors and his fellow artists began to acknowledge his work. As the critic Gustave Geffroy hailed his paintings as 'fiery and naïve, austere and subtle', and predicted 'he will end up in the Louvre', Cézanne enjoyed a one-man show in Paris in 1895 and other works exhibited in Germany and Belgium in 1900. His inheritance and his return to Provence did not solve all his problems, however: even in the peaceful seclusion of Jas de Bouffan he would agonize for hours over a single brushstroke, frequently rejecting a painting or simply leaving it unfinished if it did not meet his exacting standards.

The family home at Aix continued to inspire Cézanne and led to works such as 'The Lake at Jas de Bouffan' (above). But when his mother died the painter moved to the Chemin des Lauves and began to create his own, intimate garden filled with quiet, private places (opposite).

In 1901, sixty-two years old and at the height of his creativity, Cézanne bought a steeply sloping piece of land on the Chemin des Lauves overlooking Aix. His family's estate at Jas de Bouffan had been sold two years earlier after the death of his mother and Cézanne now could afford a new home and garden. He commissioned

the building of an apartment and studio, the studio being equipped with a 10 ft (3 m) slit in the wall so that he could pass his paintings through the wall to be better viewed in the daylight of the terrace outside.

Once the building work was completed, Cézanne turned to the garden. A high stone wall hid the studio and garden from the road and within this private space he began to create his own private paradise.

The popular private gardens of the late nineteenth century, with their trimmed lawns and gaudy bedding plants, were neat and formal. Their owners were also reaping the benefits of a technological revolution which had made available mass-produced metal trainers, treillage pillars for climbing roses, portable rubber hoses and rotary mowers. 'A strong boy can work the largest size without assistance,' promised one manufacturer while acknowledging that the Patented Anglo-American Pony Lawn Mowers were 'splendid on level or undulating ground'. There were changes in plant fashions, too: large commercial greenhouses were beginning to offer a wide selection of tender perennials and, since colour printing was still in its infancy, seedsmen used their catalogues and a combination of purple prose, fine line drawings and long testimonials ('The helichrysums I had from you last year were the finest I ever grew') to market their blowsy, 'super double' petunias, 'Giant French' asters, 'new Giant mignonette' and other horticultural marvels.

However, Cézanne, like his gardening friends Renoir and Pissarro, disliked the formal gardens of

For Cézanne, his home and the Provençal landscape that surrounded it became the focus of his work. Every day the industrious artist would leave by the front door, framed by its fig and Judas trees (above) and walk out to paint his beloved Mont Ste-Victoire. When the sun became too hot he would return to work in the cool of his garden (opposite).

the suburban middle classes, preferring an untamed, wilderness-like garden. 'Nature,' he wrote, 'is not on the surface; it is in the depths. Colours are the surface expression of this depth. They grow up from the roots of the world. They are its life, the life of ideas.' He left his lawns unmown and allowed his borders to overflow with shaggy shrubs.

Protected from northerly winds and benefiting from frost-free winters and early spring temperatures, his garden gradually filled with flowering trees and berry-bearing shrubs: the dazzling white of the horse chestnut, the pink blossom of the Judas tree; borders of dark-green Japanese hakonechloa grass and the white, blue and purple flowers of shade-loving hostas. He created leafy tunnels and labyrinthine tracks which ran through his woodland garden and he gave himself resting places, made from flat stone slabs supported by rough squared stones, setting them down among the flagstone paths which wound through the garden. Here he could sit and enjoy the scent of mock orange (philadelphus), thyme and rosemary mingling with the resinous aroma of the pine trees. The peace and tranquillity of the place

was especially important to the artist who needed the sanctuary of a garden to help him overcome intermittent depressive moods.

As he worked at Chemin des Lauves Cézanne gradually distanced himself from the Impressionists and what he called 'the Sunday celebration of the moment', and instead tried to capture the unchanging essence of nature. He studiously omitted personal or contemporary details from these paintings so that the observer would see only the 'eternal truth behind appearance'. Mont Ste-Victoire, which stood a short distance from Aix-en-Provence, finally became his favourite subject. Cézanne regarded the low hill as one of the most outstanding scenes in Provence and he painted it more than a hundred times both in oils and watercolours. 'I proceed very slowly,' he wrote, 'for nature reveals herself to me in very complex form and constant progress must be made. One must express oneself with distinction and strength.'

In 1906, four years after moving to Chemin des Lauves, Cézanne was caught in a storm while out on one of his painting trips. He died from pneumonia a week later. A year later, in 1907, the Paris Salon, which had consistently rejected his paintings during his lifetime, mounted a major retrospective of his work. It was an unparalleled success.

J o a q u í n

S o r o l l a

(1 8 6 3 – 1 9 2 3)

The name of Joaquín Sorolla y Bastida was on everyone's lips in Madrid at the turn of the century. This was the artist whose New York show was attracting an average of 5000 visitors a day in 1909 and who was being fêted as the new Spanish Impressionist. Not yet fifty years old, Sorolla seemed destined to go down in art history alongside fellow countrymen such as Goya and Velázquez. The industrious and sought after painter, juggling his many commissions, worked hard and fast – in one four-year period he created more than 500 of his luministic paintings.

His walled patio garden in Madrid served as both a retreat and an open-air studio and, preferring to paint out of doors, he would often work here. Early in the day, before the sun became too hot, he could paint, standing his easel on the tiled garden floor beneath the ochre-coloured walls of his studio. By mid morning, when the sun fell full on the garden, he might withdraw beneath the stone colonnades of an adjoining arbour and continue painting under the scented shade of old-fashioned roses and wisteria. In the evening he would review his work, resting on one of his long tiled benches surrounded by the sounds of birds in the myrtle trees and water falling from the fountains.

Sorolla created his contemporary fragrant and fountain-filled garden around 1912, but the framework for its design lay with the Moorish masters of Spain's past. The Muslims had crossed into Spain from Morocco and North Africa in AD711 and had remained there until, during the fifteenth-century Reconquista, they were finally defeated by Christian forces. In 1492 the last of the Nasrid rulers, Boabdil, surrendered the

In his art, the Spanish painter Joaquín Sorolla looked and learned from contemporary Impressionism. For his garden, however, Sorolla looked back to the traditions and techniques of the Spanish Muslims to create his cool haven from the hot streets of Madrid (left).

keys of the city of Granada and left with his retinue by the pass known for ever more as El Ultimo Suspiro del Moro, the Moor's last sigh. (According to legend, Boabdil's mother berated him: 'You do well to weep like a woman for what you failed to defend like a man.') But the sighs of regret sounded on both sides of the religious divide: for six centuries the citizens of the southern Andalucían cities of Cádiz, Málaga, Seville, Córdoba and Granada had prospered under the cultured and relatively settled period of Muslim rule.

The Muslims were a deeply religious desert people who used water, shade, palms and pomegranates to recreate the Islamic concept of a paradise on earth. Fatalistic and reflective, they constructed buildings and gardens that were as light and spacious as they were elegant. They decorated their palaces with intricate plasterwork or *sebka* which hung from the walls and ceilings like petrified lace; they extended the graceful Hand of Fatima to their visitors as an Islamic symbol of welcome and sympathy; and they created clever water features within the cloistered courtyards to irrigate small orchards of citrus trees. Long after Boabdil's departure, the Mudéjar, Muslim craftspeople who remained in Spain working under their new Christian rulers, carried these concepts forward until every country farmhouse and villa seemed to be touched by the gift of the Moorish garden. These enclosed *patio*s and *carmenes* became almost subordinate to their gardens, which overflowed with bougainvillea, jasmine and the honey-sharp scent of orange blossom, where giant earthenware wine containers, or *tinajas*, were filled with flowers and where stucco and paint brightened the inside walls of sunken flower beds. When Joaquín Sorolla came to construct his own earthly paradise garden in Madrid, it was features such as these that inspired the successful artist.

Sorolla was not a *madrileño*. Born in Valencia in February 1863, he was a child of the Levant, that bright-lit, rich alluvial plain that runs down to Spain's Mediterranean Orange Blossom Coast. Sorolla was orphaned at the age of two and raised by his uncle and aunt, a couple who were quick to appreciate that the child had an artistic gift. When he was fifteen, Sorolla was enrolled at Valencia's fine art academy where he was soon receiving prizes for his work and, more importantly, where he found the support of a patron, García. It was his patron's pesetas that gave Sorolla the opportunity to leave Valencia and visit the Prado Gallery in Madrid, where he could study and copy the Spanish masters such as Velázquez and his fellow Valencian, José Ribera.

Sorolla became convinced that naturalism and light would prove to be the keys to the art of the new century. The sparkle and effervescence which he gave to the paintings of his own garden (above) brought him fame and acclaim.

Sorolla was a young man, still in his early twenties, when he submitted his historical painting, 'The Second of May', to the Madrid Exhibition of 1884. Depicting the noble *madrileños* in their valiant but doomed attack on the invading French in 1808, it captured the mood of the moment and earned him more prizes and acclaim. 'The Second of May' also persuaded the Valencian authorities to grant him a travel scholarship to study the Italian masters in Rome, but for Sorolla this opportunity was to be a journey of discovery, not of the grand Italian style, but of Impressionism.

Just over a decade had passed since the critics had vilified the Impressionists' first Paris exhibition; now that the new movement had gathered momentum, Impressionism was fast approaching the height of its influence. Sorolla was captivated by it. He travelled to Paris to see the work of the Impressionists at first hand and returned home to Spain convinced that naturalism and light were the keys to the art of the future.

Sorolla was a realist who believed that the artist should look for his subjects in everyday life. Being a Valencian, he was never short of material. By day his city was immersed in the dazzling light of the Mediterranean; by night during the Fallas festival, the city was lit by the flames of the *cremá*, or bonfires, of pasteboard carnival floats being burned. The Levant was the most densely populated agricultural region in Spain. The rice fields of La Albufera, source of the staple Valencian dish, paella, stretched south of the city, while behind it lay the

fertile hinterland, La Huerta, still watered by an irrigation system inherited from first the Roman and then the Moorish engineers. Throughout this rich and fertile countryside, the farmers and their families laboured over their harvests of rice, carob, almond, olives, grapes, dates, oranges and lemons. Sorolla painted them all. But it was the Costa del Azahar, the Orange Blossom Coast, which really fired the artist's eye, here where the sunlight sparkled on the Mediterranean and the turn-of-the-century *madrileños* in their white linen and cotton suits gathered beneath the shade of their parasols to see and be seen.

When Sorolla returned from Italy in 1889 he and his family (he had married his patron's daughter) moved to Madrid. Sorolla submitted his paintings of Valencia's sunlit shores and sparkling seas to be shown in Madrid and Paris, pictures which prompted one critic to remark: 'This is not Impressionism, but it is incredibly impressive.' His pictures of ordinary Valencians, his

Sorolla's growing reputation gave him the means to create a perfect city garden in the heart of Madrid (above). The house was finished in 1910 and the garden, with its citrus trees and palms, its pots of cyclamen and aspidistras, two years later.

portraits (among others he painted the Spanish king, the United States president William Howard Taft and the American society figure Louis Comfort Tiffany) and most of all his capacity for capturing the Valencian light earned him international renown. Within twenty years Sorolla had shown his work at exhibitions in Munich, Vienna and London. The London exhibition caught the attention of Archer Milton Huntingdon, founder of the newly established Hispanic Society of America, and Sorolla's growing reputation in the United States and South America was rapidly advanced by exhibitions in New York, Boston, Buffalo, Chicago and St Louis.

It was around this time that Sorolla conceived plans for a house and garden in Madrid. The house was built between 1910 and 1911 close to the centre of the capital in the Almagro quarter, and in 1912 the artist laid out his two interconnected gardens. Notoriously difficult to design, small town gardens inevitably run the risk of outgrowing their designs and becoming claustrophobic and overcrowded. Sorolla solved the problem by basing his ideas on two of Spain's classic Muslim gardens, the Alcázar in Seville and the Generalife Gardens at the Alhambra in Granada.

The artist captured on canvas the chiaroscuro effect he had created in his Madrid garden (above). From its fountains and falling water to its clipped hedges and azulejos *– glazed tiles – used to decorate the benches and pools, Sorolla's garden was filled with popular arabesque features (right).*

The Alcázar Palace, built at least 300 years before Boabdil's ignominious retreat, is Spain's largest surviving Moorish garden. Although most of it was destroyed after the Moors departed, it was reconstructed by Mudéjar craftsmen in the Moorish style, with low pools set in the centre of stately, arcaded courtyards and clipped hedges separating the gardens into geometric shapes. Other arabesque features included tiled benches, cypresses and citrus trees, fountains and the distinctive *azulejos* or glazed tiles. Since the Koran forbade the representation of animals or people in architectural ornamentation, the resourceful Muslims had turned to their ceramicists for decorative ideas. Unglazed tiles had been used in southern Europe since Roman times, but the Muslim ceramicists, and especially the *malagueños*, turned the craft into an art form. Migrant Muslim potters and painters had settled in Málaga, where they employed their jealously guarded secret recipes for the metallic glazings to produce the iridescent *azulejos* which eventually found their way into almost every private and public garden in southern Spain. The tiles featured again in the 'Garden of the Architect', the Generalife Gardens built in the mid thirteenth century overlooking the city of Granada. The Generalife was designed to serve as the sultans' summer palace: jets of water fountained over canals, bubbling basins overflowed into tiled pools and reflective reservoirs stood under the shade of cypress trees among hedges of trimmed myrtle and the scent of citrus blossom. Moorish gardens such as these were reputed to grow a wide flora including roses, jasmine, arum lilies, irises, narcissi, and herbs such as mint, marjoram, lavender and thyme.

Sorolla, too, adopted both the flowers and the features of the Moorish gardens – the *azulejos*, fountains, pools and shade – for his own garden. In the first area he built two tiled benches at either end of a rectangular space, separating them by a long water feature with two fountains and two pools connected by a narrow, tiled rill. Jets of water played against the rill and splashed against the terracotta pots of capsicums and

pelargoniums which stood, carefully composed, on either side. Neatly clipped box hedges, with tiled paths and stands of myrtles, apples, plums and cherry trees between them, enclosed the area.

In the second part of the garden Sorolla set another fountain to feed a large and limpid pool which, like the traditional courtyard reservoir or *alberca*, caught the shimmering reflections of the trees above. The borders of the pool were edged with narrow bands of white and blue tiles, these *verduguillos* being continued along the border edgings, while a path patterned with tiles and rounded river pebbles set in cement linked the pool to the arbour supported by its slender stone colonnades. To complete the picture, Sorolla set sculptures, many of them his own work, among the sycamores, acacias, magnolias, jasmine, acanthus, daffodils, irises and ferns which grew in the flower beds.

The garden was still in progress when the Hispanic Society gave Sorolla his most challenging commission: a series of canvases depicting the regions of Spain. The series, still on view at the Hispanic Society in New York, was an exhausting assignment which took Sorolla eight years to complete. A year later he suffered a stroke and was forced to stop painting. Three years later, in 1923, Sorolla died. He was sixty-one. Although he had been hailed as the greatest Spanish artist of the twentieth century, Sorolla's fame began to diminish after his death. Critics found fault with his faith in Impressionism when a new order of -isms – Cubism, Expressionism and finally Modernism – had overtaken the art world and although there were signs of a Sorolla revival, especially in the United Sates, his name was gradually disappearing from the art histories of the twentieth century. In his Madrid garden, however, where the Moorish fountains played against the *azulejos* and the cherry blossom bloomed again, his memory lived on. In 1932 Clotilde, Sorolla's wife, presented the house and garden to the Spanish state and it became the Museo Sorolla.

Sorolla drew his inspiration from two of Spain's greatest gardens, the Alcazar in Seville and the Generalife Gardens at the Alhambra in Granada. He did not live to enjoy it for very long, however, and died in 1923 after completing an exhausting commission for the Hispanic Society in New York.

John James

Audubon

(1785–1851)

If the artist John James Audubon were to try to walk around his old garden, Minnie's Land, today he would find himself dodging the traffic and pacing the sidewalks of upper Manhattan. But it would come as no surprise to the early nineteenth-century artist that his garden was now buried somewhere beneath the streets of New York.

Audubon was a pioneering naturalist who witnessed the American wilderness slipping away. He was worried by what he saw. 'I like Nature,' he once declared with conviction. In 1843, even as he took part in one of the savage and ultimately disastrous buffalo hunts, he wrote: 'Immense numbers are murdered almost daily on these boundless wastes called prairies. This cannot last. Before many years the buffalo, like the great auk, will have disappeared. Surely this should not be permitted.'

When the artist finally found success in his fifties, he bought a 35 acre (14 ha) plot on the Hudson river in Carmansville, later known as Washington Heights, and built a simple, spacious wooden house with a high portico running the length of the house facing the river. Aside from one final journey to draw and paint in the wilderness, Audubon remained here at Minnie's Land for the last eleven years of his life. The place suited him well: the garden's mature elms and oaks attracted the wild birds that he had painted since childhood and he planted a further 200 fruit trees and shrubs, including pears, apples, quinces, apricots, vines and nectarines which brought yet more birds into the garden. He would draw them as he drew the fruits, berries, flowers and foliage that grew in the garden and the family of animals, including deer, elk, moose, bears and foxes, housed in his private zoo.

The pioneering naturalist John James Audubon had little formal artistic training, and yet he eventually found success as the artist and author of The Birds of America. *Many of the pictures that would later establish his reputation were drawn in Louisiana (left).*

Audubon, however, was not an artist who spent his time quietly painting and nurturing his garden, but a restless individual who lived in fear of financial ruin, told improbable tales of his past and who, but for the support of his wife, Lucy, would have died in obscurity in some debtor's jail. Instead he became the man famously responsible for his masterpiece, *The Birds of America*, and the first artist to depict life-sized birds and animals in their natural surroundings.

John James Audubon might seem a curious choice for inclusion in a book about artists and their gardens. Not a single one of his gardens survives; although he expressed regret about leaving his gardens behind, he wrote precious little about their composition or cultivation; and while his work was informed by his own careful study of plants, he was more preoccupied with his birds and mammals than he was by the native flora. After his death, however, a host of environmental and conservation organizations was founded in his name – his legacy, in the end, was a lesson for all our futures.

Despite claims to the contrary (Audubon even suggested he was the lost Dauphin, the son of the king

Summer or Wood Duck.
ANAS SPONSA. L
1. 2. Males 3. 4. Females.

of France, Louis XVI), he was born in Les Cayes, Haiti, in 1785, the illegitimate son of a French ship owner and his mistress, Jeanne Rabin, who died when Audubon was six months old. His father, who traded for a company in Nantes, France, took the child home to Nantes and had him adopted by his wife, Anne. They called him, confusingly, Jean-Jacques Fougère.

By 1790 the family had settled just outside Nantes where the child would play in the family's fruit and vegetable garden. Beyond the garden, however, France was in turmoil. July 1789 saw the Republicans storming the Bastille at the start of the French Revolution. Nantes, formerly a loyalist stronghold, suffered its own reign of terror as the local people of the Vendée, including one of Audubon's aunts who was dragged through the streets, were routinely guillotined or drowned in the Loire.

Captain Audubon had bought a farmhouse in the United States, Mill Grove in Pennsylvania, and eventually the artist was sent there to keep an eye on his father's property. By then Audubon had spent a year at a French military academy and, he claimed, studied at the Paris *atelier* of Jacques Louis David, the distinguished teacher and propagandist painter whose works demonstrated a perceptive understanding of colour and light. If he did study at the *atelier*, Audubon would have gained valuable lessons as an artist; if he did not it was all the more to his credit for, apart from a few lessons from an itinerant painter in the United States, he would receive no other formal training as an artist.

Audubon met his English neighbour, Lucy Bakewell, at Mill Grove in 1803. The couple were engaged, but waited another three years before they could marry, during which time Audubon journeyed back to France and returned to America only to lose Mill Grove in a property deal. It was the first of a succession of business failures, in Louisville, Mississippi, New Orleans and Henderson, Kentucky that, in 1819, led the artist to the debtor's prison. On his release his family rented a house in Louisville while Audubon scraped a living doing five-dollar charcoal portraits. He and Lucy moved to Cincinnati where he worked as a taxidermist, but even here his luck, and the work, ran out. 'Without a dollar in the world, bereft of all revenues beyond my personal talent and acquirements, I left my dear log house, my delightful garden and orchards and with that heaviest of heavy burdens, a heavy heart, I turned my face towards Louisville.'

His 'personal talents and acquirements', however, were not to be underestimated. Ever since his childhood in France, Audubon had painted birds in the wild and now his portfolio of wild American birds was growing. His father had impressed upon him that 'nothing in the world possessing life and animation was easy to imitate and as I grew older he hoped I would become more and more alive to this.' On the contrary, the artist concentrated on his craft. He developed a method of wiring the bodies of freshly killed birds in authentic poses, a technique that gave his pictures a tense and dramatic realism. His masterful use of botanical designs as backgrounds added to the effect, and Audubon often employed artistic licence to portray plants for their rich colour or striking shape rather than to represent an actual habitat.

His artistic preoccupations, however, did not help his various businesses. In 1810 he and a business

Audubon's masterful collection, The Birds of America, *was finally published in the early nineteenth century. One page (left) shows the summer or wood duck perched on the branches of the button wood tree (*Platanus occidentalis, *above). Audubon's attention to detail when depicting both the birds and their backgrounds captured the public imagination.*

partner set off down the Ohio river to deliver a boat-load of whiskey, gunpowder and other supplies. While the journey's delays frustrated his partner, Audubon was delighted by the opportunity to collect new specimens. At one point he joined an Indian hunting party looking for wild swans; at another, when ice on the river imprisoned the boat, Audubon settled to sketch the wild bears, wolves, deer, cougars and wild turkeys.

Ten years later, as he left his 'dear log house' and 'delightful garden', Audubon determined to concentrate on his pictures. With the family settled in Louisville, Audubon embarked on another specimen-collecting journey along the Ohio and Mississippi rivers, taking with him a thirteen-year-old boy, Joseph Mason. The two of them landed in New Orleans in 1821 and for the next four years, while Mason was taught how to paint some of the floral backgrounds, Audubon concentrated on his bird studies. He also earned a living painting portraits and teaching students, not always with success – he spent four months in the service of one family at Oakley Plantation, Louisiana only to be dismissed on the grounds that his student had become 'infatuated with her thirty-six-year-old drawing master'. It did not matter greatly to Audubon, who found another thirty new birds to paint in the woods around Oakley Plantation. 'The rich magnolia covered with its odoriferous blossoms, the holly, the beech, the tall yellow poplar, the hilly ground, even the red clay I looked at with amazement, and such entire change in so short a time appears often supernatural, and surrounded once more by thousands of warblers and thrushes, I enjoy Nature,' he declared.

In the 1820s, dogged by business failures, Audubon determined to concentrate on his last hope for success: his book. He found no less than thirty new birds in the wild Louisiana woods (above) to add to his collection.

Some of Audubon's most reliable sources of information about the natural world were gleaned from

those guardians of the wild, the American Indians. Although many tribes grew crops of marrows, beans, maize and maypop or passion flower, they possessed no word for the European garden, literally an enclosure. (A Canadian Indian described how his people would plant their crops, burying a large fish for fertilizer in a mound of loose earth and sowing corn in the centre and squash seeds on the sides. When the corn was knee high, the corn stalks supported a crop of beans while the squash leaves kept the weeds down. After the plot was harvested, the ground was left to recover and a new mound made in a different place.) To the Indians, fencing off a plot of land in the wilderness amounted almost to an act of profanity. Audubon, even as he fenced his own gardens, was aware of the ways of the Indians and their sustainable management of the wilderness. Often, his was a lone voice in their defence. Riding a train to Florida from Charleston in the 1830s he observed the grim consequences of government policy for dealing with local Indians 'confined in irons preparatory to leaving for ever the land of their birth. Some miles onwards we overtook about two thousand of these once owners of the Forests, marching towards this place under an escort of Rangers and militia, destined for distant lands, unknown to them, and where alas, their future and later days must be spent in the deepest sorrows, affliction and perhaps even physical want. All formed such a picture as I hope I will never again witness in reality.'

In the 1820s the artist was experiencing his own problems, but then, at the age of thirty-five, he hit upon an idea: he would select the best of his growing stock of finely observed and detailed bird paintings and have them engraved full size on copper plates and

Audubon painted portraits and lived in as the art tutor at Oakley Plantation (above) to support his family.

It was during this period that he came into his full powers as a painter of birds and a master of design.

printed. He would hand-colour the black and white plates and offer them for sale as prints bound into books that could be sold as collectors' volumes. The British were the only printers to whom he could entrust the work and with Lucy's help – she had set up a private school near Bayou Sara in Louisiana – he raised the necessary funds and sailed for Liverpool with more than 400 of his drawings. For the next twelve years he laboured over *The Birds of America*, overseeing the engravings, touring Europe in search of subscribers and undertaking journeys to seek out new specimens in South Carolina and the wilds of Florida. By 1838 he had achieved his ambition: *The Birds of America*, which featured 435 prints of 457 species of birds, was complete. The four-volume sets of prints sold for around $1000 a set – a century later they were fetching $200,000 – and the plates, to avoid having to give free copies to English libraries under copyright law, were published without any text. A separate ornithological biography describing the pictures and including Audubon's observations on life in America was published later.

John James Audubon was famous and the fruits of his fame took the family to New York. In 1840 they settled at Minnie's Land. The artist continued to work his customary fourteen hours a day as he managed his garden and oversaw two new projects, a smaller, more accessible volume of *The Birds of America* and a book on American quadrupeds with his friend and collaborator, the Reverend John Bachman from Charleston, South Carolina and with his sons John Woodhouse and Victor Gifford. Audubon's sons completed work on *The Viviparous Quadrupeds of North America* after their father fell ill.

When Audubon died on 27 January 1851, he was acclaimed as one of the twelve most notable Americans. His name was to live on, not only in the state of Iowa, where they named a county after him, but, even more appropriately, in all the conservation organizations dedicated to his memory.

*Audubon's home and garden have long disappeared under the tarmac, but fortunately his work survives. 'Carolina Parrots in a Cuckle Burr' (oppposite) and 'Blue Green Warbler in a Spanish Mulberry' (above left) seen alongside a branch of the actual plant (*Callicarpa americana*, above right) exemplify his powers of observation that underpinned the success of* The Birds of America.

PLATE 26
Carolina Parrot
Males 1. F. 2. Young 3.
PSITTACUS CAROLINENSIS.
Plant Vulgo Cuckle Burr

K i m

O n d a a t j e

(1 9 2 8 –)

The contemporary Canadian artist Kim Ondaatje is a committed environmentalist. While her paintings reveal little of life in her organic garden at Blueroof Farm in the lake district north of Kingston, Ontario, the garden reveals much about the artist. 'I've always been intrigued by that which we do not entirely know or understand. I prefer understatement to overstatement and really do not care for either art or gardens with a message. My industrial landscapes, for example, aren't anti-pollution paintings. When I did them I was simply intrigued by these geometrical shapes, the mystery of not knowing what goes on inside them and the beautiful movements of smoke or steam dispersing into the air and creating a misty atmosphere around the factory. These days, however, I think of my four-acre garden as my final canvas.'

Blueroof's tame wild garden, as she calls it, has its own mysteries. In the autumn, as the temperature begins to fall, dawn mists rise from the lakes and gradually disperse behind the lilies and chrysanthemums along their banks. Branches, hung with dew-dropped spiders' webs, lean out over a pond where an untethered red canoe floats free in the water. A curving line of gravestones lies under the cathedral-like canopy of a maple wood, marking a pathway edged with hostas and ferns.

Winter brings another dimension. In 1998 an ice storm drizzled and froze for several days until every blade of grass was sheathed in ice. Telephone and hydro lines failed and Blueroof fell silent except for the sudden rifle-shot of tree limbs breaking under the weight of the ice and the muffled thud as they hit the ground.

Canada's Kim Ondaatje, artist and organic gardener, stands beside a clematis in her garden at Blueroof Farm (above), where every window frames a different view: 'I think of my four-acre garden as my final canvas,' she says. The planting of day lilies (hemerocallis) and phlox around Orser Pond (left) reveal an artist's eye.

When a soldier finally broke through the debris, he asked Kim Ondaatje if there was anything she needed. 'Yes,' she pleaded, 'bring me rolls of film, plenty of film.'

Every farmhouse window frames a different view – a distant blur of blue and green spruce, a cascading waterfall encircled by cedars, a reflecting pond cradled by rocks and surrounded by evergreens. A blue jay's view of Blueroof looks down on the house with its eponymous roof and a garden that flows along the natural lie of the land. In the foreground is a cache of shrubs, trees, garden corners and ponds. Orser Pond, named after the man who excavated it, is overlooked by dogwood, daffodils, weeping cherries, willows and a gazebo. The neighbouring West Pond shelters a shade garden filled with violets, hostas and ferns on one side, and a bank of sumach, which shimmers with autumn colours in the fall, on the other. The East Pond, glimpsed through a cloud of white birch, is bordered by spruce, pine, a weeping willow and a Russian olive while a small island of various grasses and bulrushes and a fan-shaped waterfall creates a focal point within it.

Beyond the farm, nestling between ribs of pink and grey bedrock, lie 50 acres (20 ha) or so of hummocky pastureland, grazed through spring and summer by a herd of red- and butterscotch-coloured cows with their calves and minder bull. Beyond that lie

another 30 acres (12 ha) of woodland, fringed with that Canadian standard bearer, the sugar maple, which bleeds into coral, corn yellow and crimson at the end of summer. Nature trails wind through the woodland, up large rocks to lookouts and down to a riverbank where they make their way between delicate hemlocks and the moss-covered boulders that edge the shore.

Kim Ondaatje is vague about the size of her holding – the dimensions of a Canadian garden bear little comparison to those, say, in most of Europe. But being deeply concerned about the environment, and

A stand of tulip flowers beside a rib of exposed bedrock in Kim Ondaatje's garden. The artist was influenced by the teachings of a Canadian Indian and is as philosophical about her garden as she is about her art. 'Nothing,' she says, 'is forever.'

having been schooled in the ways of the wild by a native Canadian, she is philosophical about its purpose: 'I love each part of my garden in a way that I love each of my six children. But if the lawns are not cut, the beds weeded and edged, the trees and shrubs trimmed, my garden could return to the wilderness within a year. Goldenrod, burdocks, chicory, bugloss, dandelions and hosts of other so-called weeds would take over and it would be a wilderness again. Nothing is forever.'

Kim Ondaatje, Betty Jane Kimbark as she was then, was born into a cultured and affluent Ontario family in 1928, where she compensated for a lonely childhood without neighbours or playmates by following the gardener around and helping him with his chores. In her early teens her father hired an Ojibway, Jack Hawk, as one of her tutors. 'When I walk the trails or take a canoe upriver, it's his words that cling to me like a burr.

He often spoke of "mother earth" and of how "we must always give back and not just take away".'

In those days Ondaatje was weighing up whether to become Canada's first woman jockey or an artist. When she grew too big for the jockey's saddle, she signed up for art college. Her father owned a printing business and when he made trips to Germany, France and England he would bring back rare etchings and engravings which were hung on the walls of their home. There were Constables, Gainsboroughs, Turners, Reynolds and Rembrandts; her favourite print of a man in a boat with lots of white space and suggestive strokes of black around it was by Whistler. But as a small child looking at these black, white and grey works of art, she simply longed for colour.

As a painter she was influenced by Canadian artists such as Yvonne McKague Housser, Paul-Emil Borduas and David Milne, and by the American, Georgia O'Keeffe. Critics have drawn parallels between the two artists, although less in their work than in the way both women valued their sense of place. 'I was always interested in Georgia's decision as a woman not to have children while I made a decision to have as many as possible. Maybe Georgia's art has been more prolific than mine as a consequence, but as a woman . . .'

Kim Ondaatje went on to become a painter, a photographer, a film maker and a teacher. By her own admission, it was never easy. When she married Michael Ondaatje, the writer who was eventually to complete his overshadowing opus, *The English Patient*, she was disowned by her disapproving mother and arrived in Toronto with a new husband, thirteen unframed canvases and an open invitation to exhibit at an outdoor exhibition. Thirty-six years old and heavily pregnant, she placed her work before the selection committee with some trepidation.

— My child, asked Allan Jarvis, then director of the National Gallery, where are you from?
— Quebec, sir.
— You studied with Morrice?
— No sir, I was expelled from art school.
— Ah, all to your credit. Any artist worth his salt gets expelled from art school.

Her paintings were accepted, nearly all were sold, and Kim Ondaatje found herself launched on her career as a painter. As she began to exhibit in Canada, the United States, what was then Yugoslavia, Poland and England, her paintings and prints found their way into public and private collections at home and abroad. Then in 1973, she and Michael discovered Blueroof Farm. 'My life, my art, my garden have all been the result of chance happenings. Sometimes I think the gods who look after me must be exhausted.'

They had spent six summers searching eastern Ontario for the right place to live when they chanced on the small, sad-looking house with its peeling white paint and bright blue roof standing behind a host of dead elm trees. In the garden the stalks of the previous year's goldenrod and burdocks swayed in the breeze. Carved out of the Canadian shield almost two centuries earlier, Blueroof was old by Canadian standards. The original log cabin, now incorporated into the farmhouse, had been built by a British soldier before he died in 1812. His widow and two of her sons still lay buried in maple woods at the back of the property. Beside them were the little graves of two children who drowned in the river and several other unmarked graves, the final resting place of river drivers who slipped and drowned in

Ondaatje's eerie 'INCO Slag Train' grew out of her interest in the structures, contours and atmosphere surrounding factory sites in Ontario. She went on to become a print maker, film maker, photographer and gardener.

a maelstrom of logs and spring waters. In the 1840s, when log rafts were being floated down the river Depot to the sawmills, one of Blueroof's rocks, chillingly known as Dead Man's Point, was notorious for causing log jams and drowning the drivers who tried to free them.

After Kim and Michael Ondaatje separated in 1980, Kim remained at Blueroof and began raising an organic beef herd. Eight years later she turned her energies towards designing the garden. A shade garden was constructed with winding paths, boardwalks, terraces and steps, lined with hostas and leading to a fernery under the shade of the old maples. A nearby rock garden was created by cleaning off a natural rib of

'Pine Cupboard' (above), the interior of a former family home, became part of Ondaatje's 'Piccadilly' series. Her fascination with geometric shape was carried on into the garden at Blueroof with structures such as the gazebo overlooking Orser Pond (right).

exposed bedrock and filling its pockets with soil and hardy rock plants. Flower beds full of perennials edged the lawns and created islands of colour within them. Near the house hanging baskets of rose-bud impatiens and trailing pelargoniums were hung from the porch ceilings, the eaves above the boardwalk deck and in the nearby birch trees. Silvered cedar rails were used to create dog stoppers at the ends of the beds and around the organic vegetable garden behind the house to protect them from Kim Ondaatje's inquisitive dalmatians. Elsewhere the dogs roamed free among the old-fashioned perennials, ornamental grasses, wild flowers and those flowering shrubs hardy enough to survive the Canadian winter.

Canada is divided into climate zones according to average temperatures and, until the north wind blows and drives the micro-climate down to Zone 3, Blueroof lies in the warmer Zone 4. Nevertheless the artist has resigned herself to regular horticultural disasters in a garden where the temperature can drop alarmingly overnight and where the chilling winds from the north can drive the mercury down to –40°C/F. Spring plantings risk late May frosts, but impatiens and tomatoes are normally planted out in the last week of May after a spring tide of snowdrops, crocuses and daffodils, and during the pretty rush of blue grape hyacinths (muscari) and pastel pink tulips that flower against a background of grey boulders. As the short Canadian summer rolls on to the fading chrysanthemums and the first frost of October, the artist hand weeds, feeds the plants with compost, sheep manure, pond weed and mineral-rich well water, and removes unwelcome bugs and caterpillars by hand rather than by chemicals.

Her organic approach arose partly from Jack Hawk's teachings and partly from reading environmental authors such as Rachel Carson and her book *Silent Spring*. 'In the early eighties I was working on a new series of prints in a graphic art studio in Toronto. As I

watched someone washing a batch of chemicals down a drain, it suddenly hit me just how many toxic substances we were using.' She left the studio that day, never to return, and decided to devote her remaining years to the environment. 'As a gardener I am totally organic – it makes it a little harder at times, but I believe in it and I have some beautiful "weeds" here and a rich carpet of grass inhabited by as many worms as the ponds have frogs.

'As a painter I have treated the four acres like a blank canvas, deciding what to do with each part, but having a strong feeling about the ultimate outcome. Each year the garden grows a little closer to what I envisaged and now, after ten years of work, I'm beginning to get that familiar feeling I have when I am close to finishing a painting. Gardening, like everything in my life, just happened naturally. Like my family, my art and my dogs, it is one of my passions and I love it in all its seasons.'

*Seasons at Blueroof: evening primroses (*Oenothera*) and silver artemisia growing among a red rose (opposite) create a tapestry of summer colour, while orange lilies and blue vetch (*Vicia cracca*) occupy a corner of this 'wild tame garden' (top) before the Canadian winter locks the garden in a world of ice (above).*

Claude

Monet

(1840–1926)

Claude Monet was the French Impressionists' greatest exponent. He was also their most famous gardener. Once, when an interviewer asked Monet about his painting studio, the painter gestured at the landscape and declared: 'That is my studio.' He had learned the art of painting *en plein air* as a boy, playing in the sand at the feet of an amateur artist, Eugène Boudin. Executing his beach scenes on the French Normandy coast at Le Havre, Boudin always worked out of doors. Monet realized that he too must quit the studio in order to capture as he wanted the evasive light and shifting tones of his subjects.

So Monet set up his easels out of doors, convinced that he could more faithfully represent what he saw by analysing the play of light, if necessary by exact scientific means. Monet learned other trade secrets. The green of the garden, a challenge for any artist, depends not only on the contrasting shades of foliage, but also on the quality of the light. The honeyed, emerald green of a Japanese quince or the citrus hues of a weeping willow, for example, will be altered by sunlight or shade. To capture this spectrum of green, painters reach for a stir of yellow and blue, perhaps with a touch of red to soften any sharpness. Claude Monet took the technique a step further, juxtaposing strokes of raw colour which the observer saw as green. Monet was 'only an eye,' remarked fellow Impressionist Paul Cézanne, 'but my God, what an eye.'

In 1866, the twenty-seven-year-old Monet finished work on an oil painting, 'Femmes au Jardin', and submitted it to a jury viewing works for an important Paris exhibition. The composition of the three young women in the painting followed the academic manners of the day. However, while the patterns on the women's dresses carried the fine detail of a photograph, Monet left the breeze-blown blossoms and the starry buttercups or daisies in the foreground vague and impressionistic. These flowers, the dappled play of light on the overhanging trees, and the sense of being out of doors on a feisty spring afternoon combined to make 'Femmes au Jardin' an unconventional picture. The selection committee regarded it as an intolerable painting executed by a rebellious young man who was a known associate of Edouard Manet (Manet's scandalous 'Le Déjeuner sur l'Herbe', depicting naked women lunching with two gentlemen in a park, had already caused a furore). They turned it down. It was a severe blow for Monet and his lover, Camille Doncieux. Camille, the model for all three women in 'Femmes au Jardin', had just borne their first son, Jean, and the family was desperately short of money.

In 1870, his paintings still being rejected by the arts establishment, Monet fled France and the Franco-Prussian war and escaped to London where he met fellow artist and refugee, Camille Pissarro. Pissarro introduced Monet to the art dealer Paul Durand-Ruel. It

Claude Monet was the father of Impressionism and the world's most renowned artist gardener. He had lived at Giverny (left) for almost three decades when he was photographed around 1910 (above). He was, said his friend Paul Cézanne, 'only an eye, but my God, what an eye.'

proved to be the most profitable introduction of his life. Durand-Ruel was to give Monet the moral and financial support that, in 1874, helped the two painters launch the Impressionists' opening show in Paris. One art critic, Louis Leroy, railed against the collection in general, and Monet's 'Impression, Soleil Levant' in particular: 'Impression,' he sneered: 'I knew it must be something like that. As I'm impressed, there must be some impression somewhere.' Leroy had inadvertently christened the movement which was to become the most significant artistic phenomenon of the century.

Twenty years later the struggling artist was looking decidedly affluent. Now he could be seen strolling around his small country estate dressed in his favourite English tweeds, the jacket cut to reveal a pastel-shade shirt, the trousers adjusted to accommodate a growing girth. On his feet he wore fine, handmade leather boots, or occasionally a more comfortable pair of local *sabots.* The once-insolvent Claude Monet had found a house, an income and a degree of respectability. He had also found a garden. After renting Le Pressoir, the old apple press in the Normandy village of Giverny, for seven years, he purchased the house and grounds, added a water garden, planted it with water lilies and began to paint them. Again and again. For the next thirty years, throughout the seasons, under every conceivable kind of light, and even when almost blinded by cataracts, Claude Monet painted his water lilies.

Monet's garden was rooted in his art, and his art was rooted in his garden. The greater success he enjoyed as an artist, the more he spent on his house and garden: here fuchsias abound and Mina lobata *clambers over the wall.*

Monet was born in Paris in 1840, but had been brought up in Le Havre where his father managed a wholesale grocery and ships' chandler business. Giverny was only about 100 kilometres (60 miles) inland

and, profitably enough from the painter's point of view, still within Normandy's patchwork countryside of little *pays* and parishes.

Monet and his second-wife-to-be, Alice Hoschedé (Camille had died in 1879) moved to Giverny at the tail end of *le floréal,* the springtime when creamy drifts of blossom filled the fruit orchards and lumbering cattle grazed knee-deep in buttercupped meadows. With summer nearly upon them, Claude and Alice set to work on the garden.

Le Pressoir was a long house with pink, roughcast walls and grey shutters. A barn stood on either side and the sloping apron of its gardens rolled down to the road outside. Passers-by who gazed through the entrance gates liked what they saw of its broad central *allée* bordered by prim flower beds and spruce and cypress trees. They did not like the expansive newcomer with his bushy, bird's-nest beard, who replaced the trees with roses and nasturtiums. Neither were they impressed by the famous artist in their midst, despite the income he generated.

At any one time Monet would have half a dozen canvases in progress, each depicting the same scene, but at different times of the day. The result was series on poplars, on haystacks, on the cathedral at Rouen and, eventually, on his beloved water lilies. 'You should know that I am absorbed by my work. These waterscapes and reflections have become an obsession. It is more than I can handle, but I none the less want to succeed in rendering what I feel,' he told his friend and biographer Gustave Geffroy. After Monet's death in 1926 critics pointed to the obsessional water lily canvases and saw the nascent signs of twentieth-century Abstract Art in the careful chaos of the brush-strokes and the skiddy mix of colour.

Monet's art was rooted in his garden, a place which inspired more than 500 paintings. His enthusiasm was shared, and fed, by Gustave Caillebotte, himself an avid gardener (see page 44). 'I'm glad you are bringing Caillebotte,' wrote another painter friend about a proposed visit by the two men: 'We'll talk gardening since Art and Literature are nonsense. Earth is the only thing that matters.'

Monet was a *bon viveur* who enjoyed fresh local produce. His horticultural passions stemmed from the domestic arrangements of every provincial French family who, then and now, tend their rows of turnips and tomatoes, peppers and beans. Monet bought a neighbouring property, mainly for its walled garden where he could oversee the vegetable forcing frames, the cellar-grown mushrooms and the cultivation of his favourite herbs, vegetables and fruit. He visited the house in the Rue du Chêne daily to select the produce

that was to be picked first thing the following morning and served at his dinner table at seven o'clock that evening, the end of his dawn to dusk working day.

No one now doubts Monet's achievements as a painter, but what of Monet the gardener? The Tuileries in Paris, designed by André Le Nôtre in the seventeenth century, symbolize the archetypal French garden, intimately allied to geometric, architectural order and neatly carpeted with a *mosaïculture* of bedding plants. Monet did lay down a geometric template at Giverny but, always the rebel and always arguing with Breuil, his gardener, who would have more space, more air, more light, let in among the plantings, Monet created a surging sea

Frequently at odds with his head gardener who wished to see more light and space let in among the plantings, Monet packed his flowers together (above). When he painted them, he concentrated, not on the botanical detail, but on the impression of colour and light.

of bloom and blossom. The plantings spilled across the hard surfaces and blurred the margins. He wedded the house to its garden with a great, green, rose-smothered terrace and then created the highly coloured panorama which was to be enjoyed from it: at one point a rambling rose vaulted up a trellis to hang in the scented air and frame the view of a cluster of poppies, lilies, violas and red-headed lupins; in another a gravel walk lay squeezed between borders of his favourite blue and white irises, white marguerites, lilies and blood-red poppies. Even the orchard grassland was seasoned with a mass of mauve, blue and red wild flowers. Monet would stride through his domain recomposing a perspective, rearranging a composition and checking that his every instruction had been faithfully carried out by the gardeners, including one whose sole responsibility was the pond and its lilies.

Monet erected a new studio to the west of the house – although he liked to perpetuate the image of the artist labouring out of doors under the elements, he customarily finished his pictures in a studio. Glasshouses were built and wagonloads of special growing compost were hauled in for his hortensia hydrangeas and rhododendrons. He encouraged his sons, Michel and Jean Pierre, with their flower collections and, when their cross-breeding experiments led to a handsome, but quite accidental poppy it was christened *Papaver moneti* by a local priest and noted botanist, Abbé Anatole Toussaint.

A Frenchman, Joseph Latour-Marliac, meanwhile, had begun cross-breeding hardy hybrid water lilies. *Nymphaea*, which had been grown for centuries in Egypt and China, had been restricted in Europe to the indigenous wild white and yellow species. Horticulturists were captivated by Marliac's new varieties, whose plate-like leaves and bright-coloured flowers floated on the surface of a pond. Monet knew their requirements well enough: an open sunny position in still water. In 1893,

Monet upset his new neighbours by cutting down the rows of trees along the garden's central allée *and replacing them with a broad arch of roses. Worse, he filled the borders with sunflowers, aconites, dahlias, loosestrife (*Lysimachia punctata*) and delphiniums and allowed nasturtiums to trail across the walkway.*

'What I need most are flowers,' declared the artist, and he and his family planted more and more flower beds. Although Monet had a taste for the unusual and the exotic, particularly when it came to water lilies, it was hosts of everyday plants such as tulips, irises and wallflowers that were the backbone of the garden stock (opposite) and which filled many of his garden scenes; above is 'Giverny, Le Printemps 1900'.

after purchasing a marshy plot of ground across the road, he built a rectangular pond and filled it with water lilies, obtaining some of his plants from Latour-Marliac. But he was dissatisfied with the result and was driven to distraction by the cloud of dust from passing traffic which settled on the pond and obscured its mirrored scenes. He paid for the public road to be resurfaced with tarmac from the start to the end of his property –

where garden matters were concerned, Monet would brook no difficulties. He enlarged the pond several times, even diverting the local river, much against local opposition, to supply the pool. The margins were planted with lilies, weeping willow, peonies, azaleas, rhododendrons, Japanese cherries and such a host of plants that, like the garden, there was always some feature to feed the artist's eye. As a finishing touch Monet built the world's most famous garden bridge, a green-painted, Japanese-style structure which arched gracefully over the pond and sheltered under a canopy that drooled mauve and white wisteria.

When, at eighty-six, Claude Monet died in the winter of 1926, he had created, not a formal French geometric garden nor the *paysager* or landscape-style garden, but the classic artist's garden, where the artist's

eye and the imagined canvas dictated the arrangement of every flower, bower and bloom. For a while after his death the gardens fell into decline, but in 1980 a spectacular restoration was completed by Gerald Van der Kemp. 'To have a truly thorough understanding of the *oeuvre* of Claude Monet, to know his mind and the sources of his imagination, to feel him living among us, it has become essential to make a pilgrimage to Giverny,' he once wrote.

To write of Giverny is to invite another thousand pilgrims into the garden and make even more difficult the opportunity for quiet reflection beside the lily ponds. But when the grey rains of a Normandy day dull the reflections and discourage day trippers, it is still possible to walk in silence beneath the dripping wisteria-hung bridge and hear echoes of the old man in his garden: 'My garden is slow work, pursued by love . . . What I need most are flowers, always, always . . . My heart is always, always at Giverny.'

Giverny and its famous Japanese bridge (right) inspired over 500 works by Monet, including 'Water Lily Pond' (above). In his turn, Monet le jardinier *inspired generations of gardeners. As one art critic put it: 'Imagine all the colours of a palette, all the notes of a fanfare: that is Monet's garden.'*

Carl

Milles

(1875–1955)

A graceful water nymph rides on the back of a dolphin while water spouts into the air from its snout. A bronze angel wearing a wristwatch is caught scratching at a mosquito bite. Jets of water rain down on a group of bronzed figures skipping across the surface of a pond. The fountain master, Carl Milles, is at play in his garden.

Milles, 'the Rubens of modern sculptors' according to one critic, was regarded as one of Sweden's foremost sculptors and, until his death in September 1955, he perfected the plastic arts of fountains and falling water in his Stockholm sculpture garden.

The flourishing twentieth-century art of sculpture for sculpture's sake, rather than for civic or religious reasons, launched the concept of the sculpture garden. Garden designers had often incorporated sculpture into historic gardens such as the seventeenth-century Isola Bella on Lake Maggiore in Italy or the eighteenth-century rococo gardens at Weikersheim Castle in Germany, but the rise of the garden devoted specifically to sculpture was relatively recent. Different sculptors responded in their different ways. Barbara Hepworth surrounded her work with dense, informal vegetation (see page 154); Isamu Noguchi created a minimalist garden for his minimalist pieces (see page 62); while Henry Moore employed the wide open spaces of the Hertfordshire countryside as a setting for his sculptures (see page 16). For Carl Milles, the paved terraces of his hillside garden at Lidingö near Stockholm provided the perfect setting for an outdoor display of his work.

In a style which reflected the Swedish Arts and Crafts reaction to opulent over-ornamentation, the Millesgården, with its fountains, pools and sculptures, used space and simple layouts to link the garden to the house. The terraced gardens were cut from the rock of a steep hillside overlooking Lake Värtan. Smaller terraces, each filled with its own little landscaped garden of trees, flowers and fountains, led off from the three main terraces. The sculptures, by both Milles and other artists, were arranged to be seen to their best advantage, placed so that they would be viewed against the water or silhouetted against the sky. The pieces shared the garden space with indigenous trees, shrubs and flowers and with architectural fragments – a single sandstone column rescued from the Stockholm Opera House and a marble portal from the city's old Hotel Rydberg. There were also examples of the Scandinavian Arts and Crafts movement: a wrought iron railing that had been designed by Milles' half-brother, Evert Milles, and a pair of wrought iron gates designed by Milles himself. Milles had his gates placed on the upper terrace and inscribed with the words of a poem by his older sister Ruth: *Lät mig verka medan dagen brinner* – Pray, let me work while the day is bright.

The fruits of his work filled the garden. On the upper terrace the black granite 'Susanna Fountain', which endorsed Milles' international reputation when it won the Grand Prix at the 1925 World Fair in Paris, was

Carl Milles built a house and garden on the slopes of a hill overlooking Lake Värtan, near Stockholm. The Millesgården became a display case for his own sculptures such as 'Susanna Fountain' (left); it was also recognized as one of the classic sculpture gardens of the West.

set in a shallow pool surrounded by red and white water lilies and overhung with trailing weeping willows. The middle terrace, lined with long granite colonnades and mature birch and fir trees, was dominated by the granite torso of 'The Sunsinger' mounted on its towering stone plinth – Milles was a perfectionist and he laboured for seven years until he was finally satisfied with 'The Sunsinger'. Two small terraces, Little Austria and Olga's Terrace, led off from the middle terrace. A copy of the Agganippe Fountain, commissioned by the Metropolitan Museum in New York and later moved to the Brookgreen Gardens outside Charleston in south Carolina, was placed on Olga's Terrace while Little Austria was laid out as a miniature version of Milles' wife's Austrian garden.

The Heavenly Staircase, a broad flight of grey granite steps, joined the middle terrace to the lower terrace, the final part of the garden completed by Milles only shortly before his death. Paved with red sandstone from Sweden's Dalarna province and designed like an Italian piazza where people would meet and mingle, it brought together the Nordic and Mediterranean cultures. Here Milles, the sculptural fountaineer, excelled himself. There was a replica of the 'St Martin Fountain', constructed for Kansas City in Missouri, USA; figures from the 'Fountain of Faith' in Virginia, USA; a Buddha-like Jonah in the mouth of a whale; a monumental sculpture fountain of Europa riding Zeus the bull and, Milles' best-known work, 'The Hand of God', a sculpture which would be recast and mounted across the world in America, Japan, Indonesia and Australia.

Like so many of his ideas, the inspiration for 'The Hand of God' came to Milles in a dream. The artist always slept with a pencil and paper ready by his bedside – 'I feel like a singer who has laid his music score on the night table – which creates enormous conflicts within me, for the melodies or the sculptural compositions struggle in my brain to come forth.'

The artist was born Carl Emil Wilhelm Andersson on midsummer eve 1875, at the Örby Estate in Lagga near Uppsala, in Sweden. His father, Emil

Milles' 'Two Dancers' stands on the upper terrace at the Millesgården (right). Deeply fond of the Italian style, Milles and his artist wife Olga Granner gradually introduced a Mediterranean feel to their Scandinavian garden.

Café

Andersson, was a Swedish military officer known to his friends as Mille, a nickname his children would eventually adopt as their own. Although he enjoyed art, literature and poetry, Milles daydreamed his way through a schooling which failed to feed his fascination for mythology, astronomy – his father taught him the rudiments of star gazing and he was rarely without a telescope later in life – and the sea. Milles was intrigued by seafaring tales and when he played truant from his tedious tutors, he would slip down to the harbour and listen to the sailors as they landed their catches. Mythology, astronomy and the sea were to become constant themes in his work.

Milles' real education began after he left school. By the age of sixteen the artist was apprenticed to a cabinet maker and carpenter, studying woodwork, carving and modelling at night school. When Milles was in his early twenties, the Swedish Society of Arts and Crafts awarded him a prize of 200 kronor and, using the money to pay for his fare, he set off for Santiago in Chile. He never reached his destination. Milles had broken his journey in Paris and he found the French capital captivating. When his savings ran out, he found work making cabinets and even coffins and started to study seriously in his free time. He visited the Louvre and spent hours among the gallery's ancient and modern sculptures, rarely making any sketches, and instead learning pieces by heart. 'In time my fingers began to move involuntarily, as if to copy them. In this way I memorized the whole of the Egyptian and Greek collections.' He studied the Jardin des Plantes' zoological collection, took anatomy classes at L'Ecole des Beaux-Arts and attended astronomy lectures given by the celebrated Camille Flammarion at the Sorbonne University. When he met Auguste Rodin, Milles persuaded the eminent sculptor to take him on as a student.

In 1900 the World Exhibition introduced the art of Asia, Africa and the Americas to the French people. Milles absorbed it all, from the imagery of the American Indians and the Indian Bodhisattva to Chinese ceramics and the pre-Columbian art which had so inspired Frida Kahlo (see page 34). Finally, he put his coffin and cabinet-making aside and, drawing on the eclectic influences of world art, Rodin and classical form, began to make small sculptures of his own – animals, dancers and street figures such as beggars and milk carriers.

Milles stayed in Paris for seven productive years. His work was accepted by the Paris Salon and, after winning the Grand Prix in 1925, he held a one-man show at the Tate Gallery in London followed by major exhibitions in Germany and the United States. In 1927 a reviewer for the *Sphere* visited the Tate exhibition and reported: 'His early work was markedly dominated by the influence of Rodin, but his more mature creations select what he wants from Greek archaism, medieval scholasticism, Renascence heroism, and baroque tortuosity, with a fine indifference.'

Milles, meanwhile, had met an Austrian portrait

Carl Milles often arranged his sculptures so that they would be viewed against water or, like 'The Hand of God' (above), stand out against the sky. Milles also had a fondness for fountains: the Triton Fountain (opposite) is framed by the loggia on the upper terrace at Millesgården.

painter, Olga Granner, and, after a secret five-year engagement, they were married. In 1906 they bought a plot of land at Lidingö, built themselves a house and studio and began to establish the garden. The couple had commissioned the architect Carl M. Bengtsson to design the house for their lakeside retreat and a water-colour by Bengtsson from 1906 depicted the barn-like, gabled manor, perched on the hill top above an almost bare garden. It took Carl and Olga Milles fifty years to transform it into a rich amalgam of plants, landscape architecture and sculpture. No sooner had the house been completed than Carl's half-brother Evert added a long pillared loggia. In 1918 *Vogue* magazine featured the loggia, described as 'one of the most picturesque gardens . . . owned by the young Swedish sculptor Carl Milles.' Black and white photographs of the time showed the pines, birch and willows as shapely young saplings, but already the loggia was draped with greenery under its roof of roman tiles. Milles placed in earth the stone steps that led up to the loggia so as to encourage plant growth in the cracks and crevices between them and he lined the hewn-stone walls which edged the loggia with clipped bushes planted in his specially designed white urns. The whole scene was reflected in the rectangular pool where, in the centre, the black granite 'Susanna Fountain' played. It was a classic Italianate scene in a classic Nordic setting.

Carl's and Olga's regular visits to Italy were to make even more of an impact on their surroundings. After the addition of the loggia the Scandinavian interiors were recreated in a neo-classical style. Inspired by the ancient mosaics of Pompeii, the couple designed and laid several mosaic floors; walls were marbled and decorated with columns and pilasters and a studio and guest room, added to the west wing as a homage to the Italian Renaissance, were decorated with arched colonnades crowned with Corinthian capitals and even a fresco depicting the Bay of Naples. Milles continued to develop his garden and work on his sculptures and

Even while working in America for twenty years, Milles maintained a constant correspondence with friends about the management of his garden back in Sweden, and organized the addition of such works as 'Angel Musicians' (left).

fountains for almost a quarter of a century until, at the age of fifty-six, his life took a new turn.

Inspired by the work of William Morris in England (see page 52), the newspaper magnate George Booth founded the Cranbrook Academy of Art at Bloomfield Hills near Detroit for students of fine arts and crafts. Milles was invited to take up the post of resident sculptor and head of Cranbrook's sculpture department. Although he had visited the States for the first time only the year before, Milles accepted the position and he and Olga moved to their new house and garden at Cranbrook. Milles remained here for the next twenty years, working with sculptors such as Duane Hanson and developing his own work: his 'Diana Fountain' was put up in Chicago (and later moved to the University of Illinois); the massive 'Peace Monument' was unveiled in St Paul, Minnesota; 'Man and Pegasus' at Des Moines, Iowa; and 'The Fountain of Faith' at the National Memorial Park, Virginia.

Yet, despite the constant stream of commissions and the stimulating atmosphere at Cranbrook, Milles' home and garden at Lidingö remained, as one of his friends put it, 'the residence of his dreams'. From faraway Michigan, he negotiated and bought neighbouring land to extend the garden at Lidingö and every year returned with Olga to spend their summers in Sweden supervising the garden's expansion. Even after 1945, when Milles became an American citizen, he kept up a constant correspondence on the planning and maintenance of the Millesgården with friends at home. Finally in 1951 Milles left America to divide his time between Rome, where the American Academy had given him a studio, and Lidingö. He died at Lidingö in 1955 and Olga laid him to rest in his Swedish garden. Before he died, Milles revealed a surreal vision of his own reincarnation: 'I will be a water lily, floating on the surface of Hacka Lake in my childhood's Uppland, where birds, swallows and darning needles hover over the granite slopes with deep forest on one side and a meadow with one or two pines growing in the crevices.'

The Italianate feel of the Millesgården was enhanced by its trees, terraces and sculptures, particularly the classically inspired 'Sunsinger' (opposite). At his death, Carl Milles was laid to rest in his own garden, near his gravity-defying statue of 'Man and Pegasus' (above).

Barbara

Hepworth

(1903–1975)

The post-war night train which steamed down from London to the south-west coast of England took many hours before it reached St Ives in Cornwall. In the 1950s and 1960s, one of the regular travellers on the long, drawn-out journey through the darkening night was the Yorkshire-born sculptor, Barbara Hepworth. Cigarette in hand, she would gaze out on the dimming view framed by the train window: the abstract silhouette of a hill, the black bulk of a farm barn and suddenly, as the train slipped into a tunnel, her own self-portrait reflected in the glass. To her travelling companions Hepworth's face, lined beyond its years, was unfamiliar, but her name, repeated by a friendly ticket inspector, inevitably brought smiles of recognition. For Barbara Hepworth was one of the first of the British abstract sculptors whose public pieces were already appearing on or alongside new buildings in London and New York.

Back in August 1939, with Britain poised on the brink of war, Hepworth lived and worked in London. 'My studio was a jumble of children, rocks, sculptures, trees, importunate flowers and washing,' she once recalled. It also had a glass roof and as people gossiped about air raids and talked of building bomb shelters in their gardens Hepworth grew increasingly anxious about living beneath a glass roof with four young children: her eldest son, Paul, had just celebrated his tenth birthday and her triplets, Simon, Rachel and Sarah, were still under five. A week before the announcement of the outbreak of hostilities, Barbara Hepworth fled the capital with her children and her second husband, the painter Ben Nicholson.

They reached their destination, St Ives,

One of Britain's first abstract sculptors, Barbara Hepworth (above, posed with 'Curved Form (Trevalgan)') worked in her garden studio in St Ives, filling her little Cornish garden with trees, flowers and her distinctive work, such as 'Torso II (Torcello)' (left), completed in 1958.

shortly after midnight in their battered little car. It was raining; the children were exhausted and Hepworth's spirits were at a low ebb. After the lush green pastures and green wooded vales of neighbouring Somerset and Devon, Cornwall looked bleak and barren. On the windswept moorland, scabrous hawthorns, stunted by the thin, granite soil, leaned away from the prevailing wind. Broken drystone walls, patterned with lichens, rambled down from the moorland margins to the coast where, at eye level with wheeling fulmars, drifts of white sea campion broke out among clifftop gorse. Less than 20 miles away from Land's End, the most westerly point on the English mainland, St Ives encircled a harbour of bobbing pilchard boats. On sunny summer days in peacetime the streets would fill with tourists, but now, as the rains swept through the maze of lanes, the town grew grey and cold under its dark slate roofs. In comparison with the cosmopolitan bustle of London, the prospect of a life in Cornwall was not promising.

Hepworth's spirits soon rose. 'Next morning I appreciated the beauty and the sense of community, and realized it would be possible to find some manual work and raise the children, and take part in community life,

which has nourished me ever since,' she would remember thirty years later. She had never seen St Ives before. And yet she would never live anywhere else again.

St Ives had its attractions. The warming waters of the Gulf Stream gave its sheltered gardens a lush, semi-tropical character. There were the rolling Atlantic breakers on its doorstep and, in contrast to fume-filled London, the place was bathed in that clear, pellucid light that had already captivated an earlier generation of artists. In the 1880s a group of painters had settled in Newlyn, 10 miles south of St Ives, and formed the Newlyn School of Painting. A second group of painters founded the St Ives Arts Club in 1888. Walter Sickert and the American James Whistler had followed in the footsteps of the precociously talented English watercolourist Joseph Turner, visiting St Ives towards the end of the nineteenth century. Then in pre-war St Ives, as the pilchard catches diminished and the fishing industry declined, a new wave of artists, Hepworth's entourage among them, moved in to turn the old net-lofts and fish cellars into studios and workshops.

For the next three years, Barbara Hepworth ran a nursery school and worked the land, double-cropping her little vegetable garden and supplementing

Since the light was good and the climate kind, many artists settled in Cornwall; few expressed themselves with the force and confidence shown in 'Two Forms (Divided Circle)' (above). Hepworth arrived in 1939 and, after she bought Trewyn with its walled garden (right), she never lived anywhere else again.

meals with field mushrooms and hedgerow salads, and mothered her children: 'three children of the same age want everything at the same time; but individually.' Only in the evenings, and in spite of complaints from neighbours about the constant sound of hammering, could she carry on with her sculpting. In 1942 the family moved to a larger house, Chy-an-Kerris, where she had studio and garden room to work. Seven years later, as she and Ben Nicholson finally drifted apart, she bought Trewyn in the centre of St Ives.

The house and its garden were a blessing. 'Here I was in the middle of St Ives with a garden, a yard to work in with sun or moon above, and dreams of large works and freedom of action. Nobody around me has ever complained of the sound of my hammer, I only have to walk 100 yards for the tools I need and I can wander about in working clothes.' Barbara Hepworth had finally found home.

She had walked by the house many times without realizing the secret garden that lay behind the walls of Trewyn. Overlooked by the spire of St Ives church, the cries of keening gulls rained down on the little walled garden and its pool of cool greenery. Even without Hepworth's extraordinary sculptures, this would have been a busy garden, bustling with its ginkgo, copper beech, turkey oak and plum trees and its springtime bulbs, spiky phormiums and Mexican shrubby salvias.

A path of Cornish granite flagstone described a figure of eight through the garden. At the top of the eight, tall trees, bamboo and shrubs shadowed the path and competed for light. A small lily pond sat at the centre of the figure of eight surrounded by gangling arbutus, a giant magnolia and spiky-headed cordyline palms. At the bottom of the figure, a small flower border crammed with fuchsias, agapanthus, Japanese anemones, geraniums and roses was set down beside a fuschia hedge and a bright white wall. The plants, like the sculptures, gave the garden an exotic, Mediterranean feel.

Hepworth's northern birthplace was a far sterner landscape. Her father, an engineer with the local authority, was responsible for the roads and bridges in the rugged West Riding of Yorkshire, 'a land of grim and wonderful contrasts' as she once called it. During school holidays she would travel with him, sketchbook in hand, listening to his explanations of how some engineering

feat had bridged a river or laid a road over some difficult terrain. In the 1960s when Hepworth was working on the monumental 'Single Form', a sculpture 20 ft (6 m) high in memory of United Nations Secretary General Dag Hammarskjöld, she would recall those early engineering lessons: 'I had to . . . bring into my mind everything my father had taught me about stress and strain and gravity and windforce.'

Hepworth the schoolgirl was a good mathematician, especially in solid geometry, although drawing, dancing, music and painting were her passions. By the age of sixteen, the resolute young woman had already set her sights on being a sculptor. At seventeen she won a scholarship to the Leeds School of Art where she would meet that other key figure in British sculpture, fellow Yorkshireman Henry Moore (see page 16). Like Moore, there followed for her a scholarship to the Royal College of Art in London and another scholarship to travel abroad – Hepworth went to Italy where she produced no work. Instead the sculptor, ever purposeful and determined, designed and served her own apprenticeship: she wandered through Florence, Siena, Lucca and Arezzo studying classical Italian art and, at the Carrara marble quarries, learned the traditional techniques of marble carving and the mechanics of lifting heavy weights.

At twenty-two, Barbara Hepworth met and married another sculptor, John Skeaping, and moved to Rome. The couple returned to London in 1926, where they lived and worked in close contact with artists such as Henry Moore and the painter Ivon Hitchens. When she met Ben Nicholson, her marriage to John Skeaping at an end, she began a round of encounters with other

Hepworth's sculptures shared their space with the semi-tropical vegetation that flourished at Trewyn, including palms, ginkgo, yucca and cordyline. The little garden provided settings for pieces as diverse as 'Figure for Landscape' (left) and 'Corymb' (above).

Seen though 'Two Forms (Divided Circle)' (above), Hepworth's garden now appears neat and well-ordered, but it used to be littered with chips of stone and wood as she worked.

The uncompromising geometry of the large bronze 'Four-square (Walkthrough)' (top) is emphasized by its contrast to more organic forms nearby and its natural setting.

contemporary artists such as Constantin Brancusi, Georges Braque, Pablo Picasso, Piet Mondrian and Sophie Taeuber-Arp. By the time she moved to St Ives, she was already on the threshold of becoming England's foremost woman sculptor.

Once settled in her new garden and studio in St Ives, Hepworth travelled around the country to the public opening of her works, increasingly, as the years went by, titled with evocative Cornish references: 'Curved Form (Trevalgan)', 'Hollow Form (Penwith)', 'Sea Form, Porthmeor'. While she enjoyed her train journeys, she was always relieved to return to the curiously un-English surrounds of her Cornish garden. She regularly opened the garden and studio to outsiders: one visitor recalled watching her work on a piece of stone in a garden which was 'carpeted with chips of wood and stone and with blocks of wood scattered around. In those days it wasn't very neat.'

Working alongside the sculptural plants in her garden, her own pure and abstract geometric pieces grew ever more monumental as new commissions came in. To the average person in the street, they were difficult to comprehend. She defined her sculpture as 'a three-dimensional projection of primitive feelings, touch, texture, size and scale, hardness and warmth, evocation and composition to move, live and love'. One of her most evocative pieces, 'Madonna and Child', was made as a memorial to her eldest son, Paul, an air force pilot killed when his plane crashed in Thailand in 1953. It was placed in the church at St Ives close to her garden.

While fellow abstract sculptor Moore's work was drawn from animate, living things, Hepworth drew inspiration from her emotions and from her local landscapes: long before she moved to Cornwall, one reviewer had drawn parallels between her clean, sweeping, geometric forms and the prehistoric stones and dolmens of Cornwall and Brittany.

For over fifty years her perceptive hands sculpted and carved with the same sensitivity with which they pruned, pared or planted the garden. 'My left hand is my thinking hand. The right is only a motor hand. This holds the hammer. The left hand, the thinking hand, must be relaxed, sensitive. The rhythms of thought pass through the fingers . . . into the stone. It is also a listening hand. It listens for basic weaknesses of

flaws in the stone; for the possibility of imminence of fractures.' Once, she accepted an invitation to draw surgeons operating on a patient's hand. She welcomed the experience: 'There you have the inanimate hand asleep and the active, conscious hand: the relation of these two was so beautiful it made me look in a new light at human faces, hands when people are talking, at the way a tree grows, and a flower.'

There are two telling photographs of Barbara Hepworth, taken forty-six years apart. In 1926 she stands beside her first husband, John Skeaping. In his workman's clothes, his brawny arms crossed, he looks confidently at the camera. In her plain, smock dress, her thick brown hair tightly tied back and her hands behind her back, Barbara Hepworth looks shy and demure, an uncertain twenty-three-year-old wondering what life will bring to her. In the second photograph, taken when she was sixty-nine, Barbara Hepworth poses beside one of her famous 'pierced' pieces. Her hands, hurting with arthritis and lined with age, rest on the rough surface of a stone and she holds the ever-present cigarette between her fingers. The crow's-feet at her eyes hint at an easy smile and the deep etched lines on her brow suggest strength and self-confidence, the look of a determined woman, proud of her life's achievements.

Three years after the portrait was made, on an evening in May, Hepworth died in a fire at Trewyn. Five years later, in accordance with her wishes, her studio and garden was given to the nation and opened to the public.

'Riverform' (above) is set beside a stand of Japanese anemones and 'Iceberg' roses at Trewyn. This sensuous work is a bronze cast of a sculpture originally carved from American walnut. Hepworth attributed the inspiration for her compositions to her emotions and her landscape. 'Perhaps what one wants to say is formed in childhood and the rest of one's life is spent in trying to say it.'

Frederick Carl

Frieseke

(1874–1939)

'As there are so few conventionalities in France, an artist can paint what he wishes. I can paint a nude in my garden or down by the fish pond and not be run out of town.' So wrote the American artist Frederick Frieseke in 1914 to justify his prolonged stay at his country garden in northern France. He might have added that his neighbour, Claude Monet, was an additional attraction.

Frieseke was a member of an expatriate colony. He lived most of his life in France and was one of a group of colourful personalities who made colourful paintings. Partly responsible for popularizing Impressionism as a fashionable style, he was also something of a celebrity in Europe and America. At the turn of the twentieth century he was exploiting the more sentimental and ornamental qualities of the style that was to become known as Decorative Impressionism, but he left behind a body of work that evoked the sunlit charms of the cottage garden. He was chiefly admired for interiors and landscapes that concentrated on the effects of dappled, flowing light, and for his paintings of women, pictures that possessed a lively, patterned, shimmering atmosphere. For Frieseke painted not only the fashionably dressed, but also the fashionably undressed, the female figure reclining languorously out of doors under a warm sun, the nude in the garden, a woman clothed only in sunlight and shadow.

In the course of a long career he obtained numerous distinctions and honours which earned him international acclaim. He was made a Chevalier of the Légion d'Honneur at the Société Nationale des Beaux-Arts in Paris; he was awarded a Gold Medal at Munich in 1906; in 1915 he received the Grand Prix for painting at the Panama-Pacific Exposition in San Francisco and a further Gold Medal from the Philadelphia Art Club in 1922. The Italians too recognized his talents: an entire room was allocated to his work at the Venice Biennale of 1909 and he featured again in 1911 at the International Exposition in Rome and the Turin World Fair a year later. His 1914 painting 'Autumn', one of a series of sensual, reclining nudes painted out of doors, received critical acclaim when it was purchased by and put on show at the Museo de Arte Moderna in Venice. While new styles and modes moved the art world forward, Frieseke, unmoved and unapologetic, continued with his Impressionist style late into the 1930s, not at all to his detriment; indeed a writer in the magazine *Art Digest* declared: 'Frieseke, internationally, is perhaps America's best-known painter.' He had become that 'best-known painter' because of a peaceful garden in Giverny, a garden that provided the studio space, the setting and the palette for so many of his images.

Studious-looking Frederick Frieseke (above) was more of a sensualist when he painted. One of America's best-known painters in the 1930s, Frieseke owed much of his success to his garden at Giverny (left), filled with acanthus, hollyhocks and black snakeroot (Cimicifuga racemosa).

In 1887 one of the early proponents of Impressionism in America, Theodore Robinson, bought a house in a country village 65 km (40 miles) north-west of Paris. By this time, and for the next sixty years, the

village, Giverny, was under siege by an army of artists. Principal among them were American painters and aspiring painters come to focus their attention on Robinson's next-door neighbour, the celebrated Claude Monet (see page 134). Monet, while still working in his garden and studios, became increasingly reclusive to avoid them. Robinson returned to the United States in 1892 and by 1906 Frederick Frieseke was renting the property; he was to live there for a decade and a half and become friendly with his famous neighbour. Robinson's house was a typically small Normandy cottage with high walls surrounding an old flower-filled garden which Frieseke's wife Sarah, known as Sadie, set about recreating and making her own.

One of the early residents of the mainly American colony to grow her own flowers was a painter called Mariquita Gill. She had cultivated white lilies, roses, hollyhocks and poppies, and Sadie Frieseke followed her lead in planning her own garden for colour and display. The white lily, *Lilium regale*, was a recent and increasingly popular introduction. Hollyhocks, on the other hand, had an established pedigree that could be traced back to the medieval walled garden. Now this flag of the cottage garden was returning to favour. 'Seedlings are far more robust than plants grown from cuttings, so that this stately flower may now adorn our gardens without the trouble of overwintering plants,' assured one seedsman in his catalogue of 1892. Trellises, another feature of the Middle Ages, were also making a comeback in the late nineteenth century and

In paintings such as 'Lilies' (opposite top), Frieseke endeavoured to capture the genteel spirit of the pre-war years in France's most famous gardening village.

Responsibility for raising the lilies (below left) or managing the crowded, busy borders (above) at Giverny fell to his wife, Sadie.

Sadie Frieseke sited her lattice frameworks, bursting with clematis, passion vines and roses, against the bright yellow walls of Theodore Robinson's house.

Since the village had become an increasingly expensive place in which to live, Sadie Frieseke cultivated her soft fruits and orchard trees, and planted her vegetables alongside, and within, the flower beds. Land prices were exorbitant and inflated, basic foodstuffs cost more than they did in Paris, and fruit was scarce. As one artist complained: 'Prices of everything have been adjusted to the American pocket.'

Frieseke, however, did not feel the pinch for he had been born into a wealthy Michigan family in Orvosso in 1874. From 1893 to 1895 he had studied at

rigid class structures and by prevailing puritanical attitudes. The young Frieseke disliked the atmosphere and in his quest for change he abandoned the New World for the Old and sailed for France in 1898.

Like many of the other American painters of his time, Frieseke settled in Paris where he could attend the Académie Julian. Here he may have been tutored by a fellow painter and American expatriate, James McNeill Whistler, a flamboyant and often aggressive personality who had set up a school in the capital. Whether or not he actually studied under Whistler, Frieseke certainly adopted Whistler's palette of subdued colouring for a while. Frieseke first visited Giverny in 1900 and in the following years stayed in Brittany and in Moret where there was another artists' colony. But it was Giverny that exercised the greatest pull on his keen imagination and in 1905, when he and Sarah O'Bryan from Philadelphia had married, the couple moved to settle there.

the Chicago Art Institute and for two years afterwards at the Art Students' League in New York. Founded in 1875 as a reaction against the outmoded and traditional outlook of the National Academy of Design, the independent art school was run on uniquely democratic lines. Students, for example, could choose the classes they wished to attend and the teachers were expected to advise only when asked. Nevertheless, New York at this time was still a city governed by strong social codes, by

Adept at using both model and setting to enhance each other, Frieseke could create striking effects. In 'Lady in a Garden' (above), the stripes of the woman's dress merge with the iris leaves, each gaining by the juxtaposition.

Impulsive, quick-thinking and highly ambitious, Frederick Frieseke was an opportunist who made the most of what the moment offered. He had a special admiration for the detailed and luxurious flower paintings of Henri Fantin-Latour and he fused Fantin-Latour's highly decorative elements with the Impressionist palette of Pierre-Auguste Renoir, whom he also held in high regard (see page 8). Strongly influenced by the sensuality of Renoir's depiction of women, Frieseke adopted a similar emphasis, focusing on the roundedness of the female body and the soft prettiness of faces tinged with a rose-like flush.

For almost twenty years after 1890, the figure

of a woman in an enclosed garden and the theme of the nude in this particular setting became a standard subject for Giverny's expatriate painters. (In one sense the theme of the nude in the garden had already been established in the village when the dancer Isadora Duncan, who had rented a small house here, would rise early each morning to dance naked on the damp grass.) Women remained the dominant theme of Frieseke's work. A fellow American painter, Karl Anderson, portrayed Frieseke at work in his secluded garden at Giverny wearing his sun hat, pince-nez, his familiar bow tie and a loose-fitting smock jacket. The painter was shown concentrating on his brushstrokes while a nude posed in the background.

But the peaceful seclusion of these garden scenes did not last and three years later, as the First World War broke out in 1914, most of the colonists fled France. At times the battles, and the German army, were so close that the thunder of their cannon fire shook the cottage windows. Yet throughout the war Frieseke, with determination and defiance, resolutely carried on painting while Sadie, equally resourceful, continued to tend her garden – paying careful attention to the place where she had buried the household silver for safekeeping. She had always been the family gardener and Frieseke himself admitted: 'I know nothing about the different kinds of gardens, nor do I ever make studies of flowers. My one idea is to reproduce flowers in sunlight . . . to produce the effect of vibration. If you are looking at a mass of flowers in the sunlight out of doors you see a sparkle of spots of different colours; then paint them in that way.'

As First World War cannon broke the calm of the Giverny countryside, Frieseke continued to paint the garden; ever practical, his wife Sadie buried the family silver in the abundant garden to keep it safe from the Germans.

Frieseke's garden inspired his palette and influenced the brilliance of his colouring. He would portray the lush density of foliage and flowers and suffuse his paintings with a warm, chlorophyll-green light. He carried the accentuated colours of garden and canvas even further when he had the house itself painted yellow and the shutters a strong green. And like his neighbour Monet, with his blue-green kitchen and yellow dining room, Frieseke painted his kitchen walls a deep blue and his living room an acid lemon yellow.

Frieseke not only worked in his secluded walled garden, but also in a second studio space which became the location for a number of his paintings. This area, which had at one time been part of a monastery, was known locally as the fish pond and stood next to the small river which flowed through Monet's garden and fed his water lily ponds. Frieseke revelled in the freedom he found to work here undisturbed, his models reclining on a robe with an accompanying parasol. Frieseke frequently used parasols as props and as compositional devices to provide him with yet another opportunity for rich and patterned colour, ablaze with warm light, and serving as both a focusing and contrasting element for the female figures beneath. The parasol also offered Frieseke a strong geometric shape to be set against the flickering colours of the flower garden.

Blue Cupid's dart (Catananche caerulea)*, tall yellow verbascum, golden oats* (Stipa gigantea) *and other ornamental grasses patterned the Friesekes' garden and added charm to his paintings. But after fourteen years as one of Monet's many American 'Givernists', Frieseke and his family finally moved away and the artist slipped into relative obscurity.*

When his subjects were clothed he painted them dressed in colourful, flowing robes and gowns – the kimono was regarded as an exotic and essential Impressionist accessory at the time – richly decorated with banded, striped or floral patterning. His female models were carefully placed where flowers and foliage repeatedly echoed and, by turns, contrasted with this decorative patterning. 'Lady in a Garden', a canvas made around 1912, was a painting that exemplified this patterning, the striped clothing emerging imperceptibly from the flower stems in the foreground. Frieseke was more than adept at achieving a delicate balance in his work, camouflaging the figure to just the right level. He manipulated his paint to create a luminous and mottled surface, skilfully bringing together the figure, the garden setting and the effects of light, fusing the three separate elements into a dazzling unity.

But above all it was the bright-lit garden at Giverny in which Frieseke revelled. As he wrote in 1912: 'It is sunshine, flowers in sunshine, girls in sunshine, the nude in sunshine, which I have been principally interested in for eight years.'

The Frieseke household finally moved away after fourteen years in Giverny and settled in Mesnil-sur-Blangy in Normandy in 1920, where Frederick concentrated on portrait painting, working in a less decorative style and with a more muted colour palette. After his death in 1939 the artist was forgotten relatively quickly but, from a life filled with activity, he left behind a record of intimate, domestic moments and a sense of that particular stillness that only the atmosphere of a French cottage garden could provide.

Gertrude

Jekyll

(1843–1932)

The towering chimneys and mullioned windows of a grey stone manor house gaze blindly down on a stone-paved terrace where creeping, rose-pink oxalis and pin cushions of London Pride (*Saxifraga umbrosa*) have colonized the flagstone cracks. The terrace, centred on a weathered sundial, is edged with a dusting of lavender and companion stands of spiny blue eryngiums, lolling lily heads and soft-leafed, silvery stachys. A water-filled rill courses down the centre of a stone-flagged path which heads away towards a romantically rose-hung pergola.

This image of an English country garden, though neither widespread nor common, has become archetypal. It is pure Jekyll and Lutyens and the direct result of the curious relationship between a frustrated artist, Gertrude Jekyll, and an enthusiastic young architect, Edwin Lutyens. Gertrude Jekyll, described in her later years as 'a dear old thing with bird's-nest hair and lilac-coloured flouncy flowing dresses', always longed to be an artist. She became instead an artist of the garden and England's best-known garden designer.

Gertrude Jekyll spent her early years in London. One of six children, she was born in 1843 to a retired Grenadier Guards captain and his wealthy wife, a banker's daughter, close to the city centre. Even in these urban surroundings the young Gertrude was developing an interest in flowers: 'I . . . made friends with the daisies in Berkeley Square and with the dandelions in the Green Park.' When the family moved into the Surrey countryside, the nine-year-old Gertrude, armed with her well-thumbed copy of the Reverend C. A. Johns' *Flowers of the Field*, not only learned to name the wild plants of the neighbourhood, but also to understand their growing preferences. Her feel for flora seemed to transcend the science of botany: she once attributed a profound mystical experience to a childhood vision of a copse carpeted with primroses.

When William Nicholson painted Gertrude Jekyll's portrait (above) she was seventy-seven years old and Britain's best-known garden designer. But for her problematic eyesight she might have become a noted artist herself; instead, gardens, including her own at Munstead Wood (left), became her canvases.

The Jekylls were cultured and affluent. Mrs Jekyll was an enthusiastic amateur painter and a keen musician who had received piano lessons from the composer Felix Mendelssohn, a family friend. Captain Jekyll was a progressive father: he saw no reason to follow the convention of educating his sons while merely schooling his daughters in domestic skills, and he encouraged Gertrude to pursue her artistic studies. At seventeen, she had enrolled at the Central School of Art in London's South Kensington. At twenty, having gained her certificate at the School, she left to tour the Aegean Isles, diligently painting portraits, landscapes and Hellenic remains. On her return she worked to develop her crafts and arts, especially inlay, gilding, carving and embroidery, always drawing on her knowledge of plants for inspiration. In 1869, after meeting the Arts and Crafts artist William Morris (see page 52), she produced a series of cushion covers embroidered with dandelions, mistletoe, pomegranates and strawberries. In 1880 her embroidery designs of periwinkles and irises were published in an embroidery handbook alongside the work of distinguished craftspeople such as Morris, Edward Burne-Jones, Walter Crane and George Aitchison.

The industrious life of Jekyll the artist and craftswoman, however, went hand in hand with that of Jekyll the gardener. Any journey with her sketchbook necessitated taking a collecting box for plants, prompting one waggish Victorian to pen the lines:

Miss Jekyll
Went up the hill
To fetch a flower she sought there
The price in town
Is half a crown
For each like root she bought there.

She had already begun designing gardens in her mid twenties. This was in the 1860s, a time when most middle-class English households employed several gardeners whose energies were devoted to raising and planting out swathes of bedding plants. Seed suppliers, who benefited from the sales of their asters, stocks, phloxes, primulas and antirrhinums, naturally supported the practice: 'We may conclude,' wrote one Victorian seedsman, 'that the prevalence of summer bedding indicates its usefulness as a sort of visible antidote to the gloom we are so often involved in by our peculiar climate.' Jekyll dismissed it as a 'dreary mixture' and found other, more creative means of making a 'visible antidote'.

Her innovative approach arose partly from her keen eye for colour. She had been schooled by an English watercolourist, Hercules Brabazon, the artist who probably introduced her to the work of the chemist, Michel-Eugène Chevreul. Chevreul, a director at the French Gobelins tapestry works, devised colour wheels to establish complementary colours, grading them into warm and cold colours and advocating the adoption of colour gradations in the flower border. After preliminary trials in the English gardens of the 1850s, his ideas were abandoned, but the perceptive Miss Jekyll recognized their potential and was to use them to great effect. Jekyll advocated keeping plants which flowered together, growing together. 'If a border is to be planted for pictorial effect, it is impossible to maintain this effect and to have the space well filled for any period longer than three months,' she pointed out. Later, she would plan herbaceous borders in three-monthly stages, filling gaps with emergency plants such as pots of lilies.

When her father died in 1876, Jekyll, then in her early thirties, fled in mourning to her sister's home in Venice. She returned determined to create a garden of her own, approaching the project, not as a trained garden designer, but as a trained artist. The chosen site was Munstead Wood in Surrey, 15 acres (6 ha) of sandy land shaped like a giant arrow head. The triangular point of the grounds was turned into a kitchen garden and plant nursery – she would draw on her own nursery to provide friends and clients with plants. Half the land was

Jekyll rarely travelled without her sketchbook, drawing, painting and recording specimens. This watercolour neatly labelled 'Iris stylosa' (above) – the winter Algerian iris now known as Iris unguicularis *– is a typical example; she did not take kindly to the Victorians' fondness for garish swathes of coloured bedding plants.*

developed as a woodland garden while the central ground was allocated to a cottage garden, complete with cottage, and a house.

Here Jekyll could experiment with adjacent plantings: no colour, she insisted, recalling Chevreul's colour wheels, stands alone, but is made more or less significant by the colours of the neighbouring plantings. She brought her painter's eye to bear on her designs, separating warm reds and oranges from cool blues and mauves, and heightening, for example, an all-blue border with a band of yellow.

Munstead Wood was her proving ground. Looking always for shape, form and composition in her plantings, she established a spring garden and, her favourite, a hidden garden with a romantic mix of wild and cultivated flowers. She built a pergola, with paths leading to it from a nuttery and a shrubbery. In deference to formality, but also to provide an earthy canvas for a fine picture, she set out an herbaceous border 200 ft (60 m) long and filled it with drifts of colour and contrast.

While most of her contemporaries regarded cottage gardens as simply the pretty product of the peasantry, she recognized their merit as a rich source of seeds and cuttings. 'They have a simple and tender charm that one may look for in vain in gardens of greater pretension,' she wrote, adding: 'The old garden flowers seem to know that there they are seen at their best.' She planted her cottage garden with roses, peonies, antirrhinums and self-seeding lupins and foxgloves.

Munstead Wood gave her the chance to get her hands dirty in the garden – 'I have built and planted a good many hundred yards of dry walling with my own hands,' she remarked with some pride. She also completed her first book, *Wood and Garden*, in 1899 and followed it with eight more titles and numerous articles for

The climbers that clothed Jekyll's pergola at Munstead Wood (above) were chosen to blend and complement each other, but it was important to her that the structure itself, revealed as the leaves fell, was attractive and practical: sturdy enough to take the weight of the planting and broad enough to make an inviting walk.

garden journals. She might have written many more had she not commissioned the companionable Edwin Lutyens to design her a house.

When they took tea together at their first meeting, Jekyll, then in her mid forties, was a forbidding figure in her matronly Victorian frock and black felt hat trimmed with feathers. But, peering myopically past the silver tea kettle at young Mr Lutyens (he was still in his late teens), she recognized his potential: she not only commissioned him to design her own house, but persuaded many of her friends to do likewise. It could be a risky undertaking. Although in the later years of their partnership he learned to accept Jekyll's restraining influence, an ambitious Lutyens plan was quite capable of bankrupting a client. He also learned to listen to her

Gertrude Jekyll's careful studies of flowers (above) and their habitats proved useful when she came to plan the flower borders of annuals, mixed perennials and shrubs at Munstead Wood (left). 'The purpose of a garden is to give happiness and repose of mind, which is more often enjoyed in the contemplation of the homely border,' she wrote.

ideas on vernacular architecture, most of them gathered from William Morris and his Arts and Crafts movement.

More than seventy properties benefited from the twenty-year collaboration between Lutyens and Jekyll, or 'Aunt Bumps, Mother of All Bulbs' as he affectionately called her. Some involved hands-on work, while some were based on sets of finely detailed plans supplied to the owners. Many were in southern England, such as the Thames-side Deanery Garden in Berkshire, and Upton Grey and Marsh Court in Hampshire, but their collaborations included locations further afield such as Lambay Island in County Dublin and Lindisfarne, Northumberland's Holy Island. In 1906 the couple approached what was to become one of their finest achievements, Hestercombe in south-west England.

In the fertile Somerset bowl Lord Portman had built for himself a grand house with views across the Blackdown Hills. The garden, in the early 1900s at least, was characterless and dull. Lutyens and Jekyll accepted the commission and, with bold layouts, transformed the place into an Elizabethan-like pleasure garden incorporating some of their favourite details – water gardens, raised walkways and sunken lawns. The plan centred on two elements, a large sunken parterre and, on a second axis, a 'Wrenaissance orangery', built as a homage to Sir Christopher Wren, the architect responsible for rebuilding St Paul's Cathedral after the Great Fire of London. The parterre and the orangery hinged on a third feature, an open stone rotunda. The geometry was exact, the details complicated and the effect exquisite.

The parterre was based on the Great Plat, where four long lawns, edged with flagstones and bordered by solid stone walls, divided the space diagonally. Lutyens employed his basic materials, stone and timber, with precision. The seductive Ham Hill stone, which came sparkling with reflected light from the local Hamdon Hill quarry, was reserved for the fine work. Rougher stone was used for pillars and paving, and

Jekyll's and Lutyens' combined talents could be inspirational. At Hestercombe, Jekyll planted silvery stachys, lavenders and yucca before the 'Wrenaissance orangery' Lutyens had designed (above), and set a clever mix of bergenia, lilies, delphiniums and scarlet oriental poppies against Lutyens' stone steps leading to the pergola (right).

coarse-textured stone for the walling. The clever business, from Jekyll's point of view, was to design subtle plantings that complemented, rather than buried, these architectural features. The plan called for her typical 'simplicity of intention, and directness of purpose'.

Clematis, Russian vine (*Fallopia baldschuanica*) and roses mounted the great oak beams of the pergola. Banks of the globe thistle, *Echinops ritro* 'Veitch's Blue', were set swaying beneath Lutyens' mellow stone balustrades. A sinuous thread of silvered stachys wound around the paving stones and the shapely, spiky stands of yucca. Elsewhere many of Jekyll's favourites such as bergenia, lavender and santolina were added, primarily for their shape and texture.

Jekyll regarded the gardener's craft as a way of 'painting a landscape with living things' and creating pictures which must work 'from all points and in all lights'. As an artist, her studious copies of the great masters such as Turner went well beyond those of the drawing-room enthusiast, but in her late forties she suffered from increasing eyesight problems, and was persuaded to consult an eminent eye specialist in Wiesbaden. The diagnosis he delivered was devastating: she was told she must abandon at once her painting and embroidery. Although she heeded the advice, she regretted it for the rest of her life. 'When I was young I was hoping to be a painter, but . . . I was obliged to abandon all hope of this . . . on account of extreme and always progressive myopia.'

Eventually her failing eyesight forced her to abandon garden design as well and when she died in 1932 the nation lost one its most influential and popular garden designers. But the woman who popularized a passion for wild and natural gardens, who advocated informality and colour gradation in the flower borders, and who warned that 'no artificial planting can ever equal that of Nature', would not be forgotten. The spirit of Gertrude Jekyll lives on.

'It should be borne in mind that a good hardy flower border cannot be made all at once,' declared Jekyll as she deployed her grey, green, white and silver scheme around Lutyens' classic steps and balustrades at Hestercombe.

Emil Nolde

(1867–1956)

Emil Nolde was one of the twentieth century's greatest exponents of the art of flower painting. He painted his flowers with such intense and vivid colours that a friend suggested he might be exaggerating the colour of nature. Nolde vigorously defended himself, explaining that when he took a finished canvas from the studio walls and stood it among the flowers themselves, his own work paled by comparison. 'We have no idea how jaded our eyes have become,' he declared. The German artist painted figures, landscapes and, repeatedly after a stormy and traumatic sea crossing in 1910, seascapes, but the most frequently occurring subjects from the beginning of his working life to the end were his flowers and his gardens.

His first mature flower paintings date from the early 1900s. They were inspired by his neighbours' cottage gardens, each a blaze of summer colour, on the Baltic island of Alsen where he had rented a fisherman's cottage near the village of Guderup. These were followed from 1916 to 1926 by paintings from a new garden at Utenwarf where he and his wife occupied an old farmhouse and in his final period at Seebüll in the garden which surrounded the house and studio he designed for himself.

Sometimes Nolde executed detailed studies of individual blooms; sometimes he would include a flower in a vase as part of a still life; occasionally he painted a garden 'portrait' where human figures were juxtaposed with burgeoning, flower-filled borders. Gustav Schiefler, one of the early collectors of his work, described the artist at work seated in his garden, surrounded by stocks, asters, pinks and carnations. As he withdrew into his work, applying one colour after another, 'subjecting the confusion of colour to the logic of form', his eyes glowed with pleasure.

Content with his isolation from the art world, Emil Nolde preferred to withdraw into his down-to-earth farm garden (left) in northern Germany. Here with his paints he was free to subject 'the confusion of colour to the logic of form'.

Introverted and isolated, Nolde had few followers and no pupils during his lifetime. Aside from his colleagues in the Brücke movement, the 'bridge' of German Expressionist painters such as Ernst Kirchner, Erich Heckel and Max Pechstein, Nolde showed no curiosity for the work of other artists of his generation. He had no great desire to exhibit his work, which, remarkably in four decades of painting, showed little stylistic change.

Emil Nolde lived through the end of the German empire, two cataclysmic world wars, economic depression and political repression; he witnessed the birth of the motor car and the death of the great French Impressionists; he outlived Kirchner and Pechstein. And yet his work seemed to be devoid of any social comment. Instead he methodically drew on his acute powers of observation to faithfully paint his immediate surroundings. His wife told the artist Paul Klee: 'He so utterly belongs to Germany.' For Nolde *die Heimat* – home – remained the primal soil.

The artist was born in 1867 on the family farm in northern Schleswig-Holstein, at Nolde near Tondern. He was christened Emil Hansen, but later in life, and as if to affirm his sense of place, changed his name to that of his birthplace. By all accounts, including his own, he enjoyed a happy childhood. His mother kept the house and garden and Nolde remembered in his autobiography how in her flower garden 'all the flowers bloomed for her pleasure and for mine, and the sun shone out over the garden.' Like any country child, he was close to his rural community and to the natural world. He even added to it, at one point planting his own small copse of maples, ashes, oaks and chestnuts, each one raised from 'the fruit of the big trees'.

He began work, not as an artist, but as a craftsman, completing a woodcarver's and draughtsman's apprenticeship in the furniture factories of Munich, Karlsruhe and Berlin. However, by the age of twenty-four, Nolde had started to teach ornamental drawing at the Museum of Industry and Crafts in St Gallen. In 1897 he began to paint full time and travelled to Paris, Copenhagen and Berlin before settling with his Danish wife Ada in their little rented cottage on the island of Alsen.

Nolde not only shared many of the aspirations of the Expressionist Brücke movement when it was formed in Dresden during 1905, he also exhibited with them in 1906 and he enjoyed the stimulation of city life and travel. Between 1913 and 1914 he embarked on an epic journey across Russia, China and Japan, finally reaching Polynesia where the vitality of the primitive sculpture made a deep impression on him.

Yet his country home on Alsen inexorably drew him back. Like Cézanne who once confessed, 'If you were born down our way, that's that: nothing else will do,' Emil Nolde found all that he needed within the lowlands of the Baltic peninsula. When in 1912 he and

Seebüll was the house Emil and Ada Nolde built. Little Seebüll (right) was its reed-thatched summerhouse and workshop. Hidden in the chaos of colour and flower was the couple's secret motif, A and E.

Ada moved to their farmhouse at Utenwarf with its marshland, its deep, straight sluice channels and its little villages of thatched houses, the cold light and the long horizons of the area inspired him. But in 1926 contractors began constructing new drainage systems in the area and their work threatened the peace of the place. Nolde and his wife left reluctantly, moving over the border into Germany, to Seebüll, where he remained for the rest of his life.

*Foxgloves (*Digitalis purpurea, *opposite) and Nolde's 'Fingerhut und Lilien' (above): stand the painting among the flowers, he would assert, and the pigments turned pale by comparison with the real thing.*

In 1934 Nolde, like thousands of his countrymen, joined the Nazi party, only to be persecuted by the party as an avant-garde painter and forbidden to paint.

Ada died of a heart attack as the war in Europe came to an end and two years later Nolde married a friend's daughter, Jolanthe Erdman. She was twenty-six, he eighty-one. Four years later Nolde was rediscovered by the arts establishment and in 1952 there was a large retrospective exhibition of his paintings, many of them inspired by the blooms and blossoms he grew at Seebüll.

Haus Seebüll was built between 1927 and 1937, a massive, purple-bricked building which stood proud of the flatlands of north Friesland, surrounded by a magnificent but mysterious flower garden. The magnificence lay in its size and richness, the mystery lay in its secret layout: when Ada and Emil came to carve out their garden from an empty field corner, 'I drew out two letters, A and E, with a bit of water as an ornament between them, linking the letters.' Visitors strolled between the flowers and vegetable beds along his private alphabet of paths, completely ignorant of the design. When friends questioned the painter about the principles which underpinned his designs, Emil gave nothing away. As he recalled later: 'We told no one. We said nothing.'

The Friesland soil is a heavy sedimentary clay laid down during the millennia when this rich land still lay beneath the sea. Emil and Ada lightened the clay with sand, drained it with ditches and sheltered the garden behind screens of tall reed beds, high hedges and trees. Once the infrastructure was in place Nolde could begin to plant his shrubs, flowers and vegetable beds, initially in the cottage-style fashion he remembered from his childhood and from their 'beautiful little garden' they had left at Utenwarf.

Within two years he was proudly telling a friend that the young garden was swelling with an abundance of flowers 'lovelier than we ever had'. The scent of the mignonettes carried into the house and his sunflowers, which he painted in a series beginning in 1926 and continuing for the next twenty years, thrived so well that they towered over his head.

As he nurtured his garden, Nolde continued to work on his own version of paradise. He built a reed-thatched summerhouse, which he called Little Seebüll, and a workshop – 'a real studio, by comparison with the wooden shed on Alsen' – later adding a second storey to house his own exhibition space. It was the fulfilment of a dream; over thirty years earlier he had confided to Ada his desire to buy a private house with a great barn

in which to hang his pictures 'so that nobody shall laugh at them or even see them, beyond the occasional stray wayfarer.'

But there were unforeseen problems: his great octagonal dwelling house, orientated towards the south-west so that it captured the full light of the sun's daily passage, showed signs of subsiding into the soft clay. The foundations had to be underpinned and a second skin of brickwork added to the outside of the house. However, these were minor inconveniences

compared to the apocalyptic clouds gathering on the political horizon. Although Nolde shared many of the nationalist aspirations of Hitler's Germany, party officials were soon removing more than a thousand of his works from German museums in a purge to rid the country of what was regarded as degenerative art. By 1941 the painter was forbidden to paint. Nolde locked himself away at Seebüll where, despite the ban on his works, he began to work in watercolour on what he called his 'unpainted pictures'. By the end of the war he had painted 1300 of them.

From the sprinkling of rose petals during *Fronleichnam* (Corpus Christi) to the harvest home festivals of a hundred different nations, flowers, especially wild flowers, have always served as significant cultural icons. None carries so much potency as the *Klatschrose*, the common poppy. Traditionally a symbol of growth, death and regeneration, the poppy has been an inseparable part of the cereal harvest since Neolithic times and only the recent, reckless use of herbicides seems to have temporarily arrested its scarlet-headed progress. But the opportunistic poppy seeds, capable of lying dormant for forty years at least, continue to germinate whenever conditions permit. This was nowhere more apparent than during Europe's two world wars when in the aftermath of some cataclysmic battle the spoiled wasteland of mud and blood would burst into a sea of poppy blooms in early summer.

In Flanders Field the poppies grow
Between the crosses, row on row,

as the Canadian poet John McRae wrote during the First World War. During the Second, Nolde too turned to the poppy, subtitling his 'Large Poppies' 'Rot, Rot, Rot' – Red, Red, Red. The painting, he would insist, was not born of calculation, but of chance. 'If I scatter seeds in my garden which then don't grow exactly as I intended, but which bloom just as beautifully . . . then I am grateful and I certainly don't uproot the flowers just because they are not exactly the way I wanted them.' Nolde, however, was profoundly aware of the significance of the seasons' swing and the repeated cycle of seed, flower, fruit and seed which he minutely observed in his own garden at Seebüll. In his autobiography he likened the life cycle of the flower – 'sprouting, blossoming, gleaming, glowing, bringing joy, drooping, wilting, ending up on the rubbish tip' – to that of his flower paintings, also subject to the immutable laws of creation and decay.

As he had once confided to Ada, he would

Earthy, everyday blooms like sunflowers (opposite) and sneezeweed (helenium) provided Nolde with the subjects for paintings such as 'Späte Blumen' (above). In the Second World War the works were classed as degenerate, so the artist began his series of 'unpainted pictures'.

have preferred to have worked in private, managing his garden and painting pictures which he would share only with those who understood them. 'Then no doubt the day would come when the art could bring unalloyed pleasure not only to isolated individuals, but to many.' Little did he know in the dark days of the early 1940s that this was to happen shortly to his own great body of work. When the Second World War came to an end and Nolde was free to paint in public again, he returned to his garden – 'first a few garden pictures with great, glowing red poppies, to get used to the colours' – and to his 'unpainted pictures', many of which he reworked in oils. (In his later years Nolde abandoned oils altogether and painted exclusively in watercolours.)

As the old battle fields of poppies bloomed and peace descended across Europe, Nolde received news from Munich that his works were to be included in an exhibition of 'Degenerate Art'. In the event Nolde exhibited more than any other artist.

By the end of the war Nolde had produced more than a thousand 'unpainted pictures'. And yet he was always more reticent about exhibiting paintings such as 'Dahlien und Wilder Wein' (above) than he was of proudly inviting friends in to admire the garden that he and Ada had created at Seebüll from an unpromising field.

Artists' Gardens is dedicated to the memory of Annik Marsollier.

Acknowledgements

I am deeply indebted to the artists and trustees for their kind co-operation, particularly to Kim Ondaatje and the late Patrick Heron and to the Henry Moore Foundation, the Isamu Noguchi Foundation, the Millesgården and the Tate Gallery at St Ives. I am also grateful to the many individuals who helped with the book, including Janet Axten, Alan Bowness, Roger Calow, Ina Cole, Robin Fields, Hannah Fleming, Chelsey Fox, Rick Goldsmith, Sandy Green, Kahlia Laws, Poppy Owen, David Petts, Jerry Ross, Michelle Seddon Harvey, Glenn Storhaug, Roy Treherne of Wyevale Garden Centres, Charu Vallabhbhai, and especially to Catherine Hervé Petts for her research, Caroline Ball for her patience, Abby for her support and to my most influential artist gardener, Peggy, for her inspiration.

I have drawn on numerous sources for this book and the following are among the many which merit further reading:
Richard Bisgrove, *The Gardens of Gertrude Jekyll*, Frances Lincoln, 1992; Jane Brown, *Gardens of a Golden Afternoon*, Allen Lane, 1982; Derek Fell, *The Impressionist Garden*, Frances Lincoln, 1997; Sally Festing, *Gertrude Jekyll*, Penguin, 1993; Buckminster Fuller, *Operating Manual for Spaceship Earth*, Amereon, 1978; Mel Gooding, *Patrick Heron*, Phaidon, 1994; A. M. Hammacher, *Barbara Hepworth*, Thames and Hudson, 1968; Barbara Hepworth, *A Pictorial Autobiography*, Moonraker Press, 1970 (Tate Gallery Publications, 1993); Barbara Hepworth Retrospective Exhibition catalogue, Whitechapel Gallery, 1954; Hayden Herrera, *Frida Kahlo: the paintings*, Bloomsbury, 1991; Penelope Hobhouse (ed.), *Gertrude Jekyll on Gardening*, National Trust/Collins, 1983; Anthony Huxley, *The Painted Garden*, Windward, 1988; Philip James (ed.), *Henry Moore on Sculpture*, Da Capo Press, 1992; Claire Joyes, *Life at Giverny*, Thames and Hudson, 1985; Andrea Kettenmann, *Frida Kahlo*, Benedikt Taschen, 1993; Vivien Knight (ed.), *Patrick Heron*, John Taylor in association with Lund Humphries, 1988; Fiona MacCarthy, *William Morris, A Life For Our Time*, Faber and Faber, 1994; Henry Moore, *My Ideas, My Inspiration, My Life as an Artist*, Ebury Press, 1986; Gillian Naylor (ed.), *William Morris By Himself*, Macdonald Orbis, 1988; Jean Renoir, *My Life, My Films*, Da Capo Press, 1991; Alan Watts, *The Way of Zen*, Pelican, 1962.

Picture Credits

Page 1, Anne Hyde. Page 2, Andrew Lawson. Page 6, Andrew Lawson. Page 8, Derek Fell. Page 9, Service Communication, Mairie de Cagnes-sur-Mer. Page 10, AKG. Page 11, Derek Fell. Page 12, Service Communication, Mairie de Cagnes-sur-Mer. Page 13, Derek Fell. Page 14 (left), Derek Fell. Page 14 (right), Service Communication, Mairie de Cagnes-sur-Mer. Page 15, The Bridgeman Art Library. Page 16, Henry Moore Foundation/Michael Furze. Page 17, Henry Moore Foundation. Page 18, Henry Moore Foundation/Michael Furze. Page 19, Henry Moore Foundation/Michael Furze. Page 20 (left), Henry Moore Foundation/Michael Furze. Page 20/1, Henry Moore Foundation/Anita Feldman Bennet. Page 22, Henry Moore Foundation/Anita Feldman Bennet. Page 23, Henry Moore Foundation/Michael Furze. Page 24/5, Henry Moore Foundation. Page 26, Condé Nast. Page 27, Bartlett Studio. Page 28, Bartlett Studio. Page 29, Condé Nast. Page 30, Condé Nast. Page 31, Bartlett Studio. Page 32, Condé Nast. Page 33, Condé Nast. Page 34, Art Resource, NY. Page 35, AKG. Page 36 (left), Museo Dolores Olmedo Patino. Page 36/7, Museo Dolores Olmedo Patino. Page 38, AKG. Page 39, Museo Dolores Olmedo Patino. Page 40, Museo Dolores Olmedo Patino. Page 41, Art Resource, NY. Page 42/3, Museo Dolores Olmedo Patino. Page 44, Giraudon. Page 45, Giraudon. Page 46, Yerres Hôtel de Ville. Page 47, Yerres Hôtel de Ville. Page 48 (left), Yerres Hôtel de Ville. Page 48 (right), Derek Fell. Page 49, Jerry Harpur Garden Library. Page 50, Giraudon. Page 51, Harry Smith Collection. Page 52, Red House/Edward Hollamby. Page 53, The Bridgeman Art Library. Page 54, Anne Hyde. Page 55, Red House/Edward Hollamby. Page 56/7 Red House/Edward Hollamby. Page 58, Red House/Edward Hollamby. Page 59, Planet Earth Pictures. Page 60, Red House/Edward Hollamby. Page 61, Red House/Edward Hollamby. Page 62, The Isamu Noguchi Foundation/Akira Takahashi. Page 63, The Isamu Noguchi Foundation/Jun Miki. Page 64 (left), The Isamu Noguchi Foundation. Page 64/5 The Isamu Noguchi Foundation/John Berens. Page 66, The Isamu Noguchi Foundation/Michio Noguchi. Page 67, The Isamu Noguchi Foundation/Shigeo Anzai. Page 68/9, The Isamu Noguchi Foundation/John Berens. Page 70, The Isamu Noguchi Foundation/Shigeo Anzai. Page 71, The Isamu Noguchi Foundation/Kevin Noble. Page 72, Patrick Heron. Page 73, Julian Feary. Page 74, Patrick Heron/DACS. Page 75, Patrick Heron. Page 76, Patrick Heron. Page 77, Patrick Heron/DACS. Page 78/9, Patrick Heron. Page 80, Patrick Heron/DACS. Page 81, Patrick Heron. Page 82, Derek Fell. Page 83, Art Resource, NY/National Portrait Gallery, Smithsonian Institute. Page 84 (left), Sotheby's NY/private collection. Page 84/5, Derek Fell. Page 86, Derek Fell. Page 87, Derek Fell. Page 88, Art Resource, NY/National Museum of American Art, Washington. Page 89, Derek Fell. Page 90/1, Derek Fell. Page 92, B & U International Picture Service. Page 93, Giraudon. Page 94/5, B & U International Picture Service. Page 96, Harry Smith Collection. Page 97, AKG. Page 98, Giraudon. Page 99, B & U International Picture Service. Page 100/1, B & U International Picture Service. Page 102, Derek Fell. Page 103, Giraudon. Page 104, Giraudon. Page 105, Derek Fell. Page 106, The Bridgeman Art Library. Page 107, Derek Fell. Page 108, Derek Fell. Page 109 (left & right), Derek Fell. Page 110, Oronoz. Page 111, Index. Page 112, Museo Sorolla. Page 113, Oronoz. Page 114, Museo Sorolla. Page 115, Oronoz. Page 116/17, Oronoz. Page 118, Louisiana State Parks. Page 119, Ann Ronan. Page 120, Audubon Museum. Page 121, A–Z Botanical. Page 122, Louisiana State Parks. Page 123, Louisiana State Parks. Page 124 (left), Audubon Museum. Page 124 (right), Harry Smith Collection. Page 125, Giraudon. Page 126, Kim Ondaatje. Page 127, Steve Behal. Page 128, Kim Ondaatje. Page 129, Kim Ondaatje/Confederation Art Centre, Charlottetown PEI. Page 130 (left), Kim Ondaatje/private collection. Page 130/1 Kim Ondaatje. Page 132, Kim Ondaatje. Page 133 (top & bottom) Kim Ondaatje. Page 134, Derek Fell. Page 135, AKG. Page 136, Andrew Lawson. Page 137, Andrew Lawson. Page 138/9, The Garden Picture Library. Page 140, AKG. Page 141, Derek Fell. Page 142 (left), AKG. Page 142/3, Andrew Lawson. Page 144, Millesgården. Page 145, Millesgården. Page 146/7 Millesgården. Page 148, Millesgården. Page 149, Millesgården. Page 150/1, Millesgården. Page 152, Millesgården. Page 153, Millesgården. Page 154, Andrew Lawson. Page 155, Ida Kar. Page 156, Andrew Lawson. Page 157, Barbara Hepworth Museum and Sculpture Garden. Page 158, Barbara Hepworth Museum and Sculpture Garden. Page 159, Barbara Hepworth Museum and Sculpture Garden. Page 160 (top), Barbara Hepworth Museum and Sculpture Garden. Page 160 (bottom), Andrew Lawson. Page 161, Andrew Lawson. Page 162, Derek Fell. Page 163, Smithsonian Institute. Page 164 (top), Terra Museum of American Art. Page 164 (bottom), Anne Hyde. Page 165, Derek Fell. Page 166, Terra Museum of American Art. Page 167, Derek Fell. Page 168, Derek Fell. Page 169, Derek Fell. Page 170, The Garden Picture Library. Page 171, The National Portrait Gallery, London. Page 172, Godalming Museum. Page 173, Andrew Lawson. Page 174/5 The Garden Picture Library. Page 175 (right), Godalming Museum. Page 176, The Garden Picture Library. Page 177, Andrew Lawson. Page 178/9, Andrew Lawson. Page 180, Stiftung Nolde Seebüll. Page 181, Stiftung Nolde Seebüll. Page 182/3 Stiftung Nolde Seebüll. Page 184, The Bridgeman Art Library. Page 185, A–Z Botanical. Page 186, Stiftung Nolde Seebüll. Page 187, AKG. Page 188 (left), AKG. Page 188/9, Stiftung Nolde Seebüll.

Index

Page numbers in *italic* refer to the illustrations